Shannon Kelly White is a neuroscientist, former nun, mountaineer and shape-shifter. Shannon also invented the wheel and those little shoes for dogs. Haha. Not really. Sadly, the only mountain she's scaled is made of skin. Plus a real one in Peru but, if she's being honest, she took the train up.

Shannon is a writer, mum, nurse and doodle-joke enthusiast. She lives in Torquay, Australia. Her blog, *Shannon's Kitchen*, began as a hobby a few years ago and her online community includes readers from across the world, all of whom are awesome and often a little weird.

Shannon is enthusiastic about healthy eating but thinks diet culture can go fuck itself. She loves delivering literary dick punches to those who misrepresent 'wellness' and perpetuate food-fear. She enjoys travelling, eating cookies and erotic massage. Shannon's Master of Nutrition studies have been told to cool their jets while she tackles the role of stay-at-home mum to two adorable, nutso children.

Shannon's life motto is: 'Withhold Thy Fucks'.

www.shannonskitchen.com

SHANNON'S KITCHEN

HEALTHY FOOD YOU'LL ACTUALLY F**KING EAT!

SHANNON KELLY WHITE

Illustrated by Evi O. and Daniel New
Photography by Michael Woods
Food Styling by Karina Duncan

Dedicated to every legendary flog who has joined me
in *Shannon's Kitchen* on the Internet Machine.

Family, friends and complete strangers.

You guys are such a pack of hilarious dickbeetles –
so funny, so open and so generous.

You have encouraged the shit out of me, you're good people.
I mean, you're bad people, but you're good people.

You know what I mean.

Thank you x

CONTENTS

BREAKFAST SHIT

SALADY SHIT

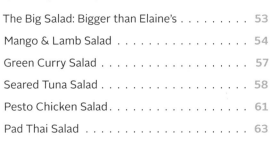

FISHY SHIT

VEGGIE SHIT

CHICKEN SHIT

MEATY SHIT

SNACKY & SWEET SHIT

HELLO
(WHO THE FUCK IS SHANNON?)

Hello. I'm Shannon and I'm a bit of a dickhead. I'm inappropriate and I curse too much and I have made thousands of penis jokes in my 34 years, even in front of my poor mum. I live in a town in Australia with Mr Shannon, our two little boys, three chooks, two dogs and one shitstain of a cat. Keeping them all alive is busy work but it fills my sooty heart with love.

I'm not just a mum and a knob; I'm also a registered nurse. I love being a nurse, even though it means I've had liquid poo splattered on my face once (yes, with an open mouth) and my leg urinated on twice. Nursing hasn't just given me unsolicited contact with other people's bodily fluids; it has also given me zero tolerance for bullshit like, for example, the sudden and meteoric rise of health bloggers who seem to think that drinking from a coconut is enough of a qualification to disseminate health advice.

It also means I give a fuck about being healthy. Because the food you eat doesn't just affect your level of hotness and associated stiffie-induction levels, it also affects the motherfucking organs inside you. Good food helps you live with energy, shit awesome shits and last the distance.

But I also discovered the healthy food world can be as appealing as having your bikini line tidied up with a high-pressure hose. It's a little overzealous. It can be obnoxious, preachy and full of fads. It's usually boring, and worst of all, it can make you feel like a real douchenozzle when you 'fail' and hook into an entire BBQ chicken and family-size block of chocolate before you've even driven away from the supermarket.

The wankers and fuck-knuckles of this community really chapped my fanny and, quite frankly, some of their recipes tasted like penis. So I started creating my own healthy recipes because healthy food isn't just for uptight dickbeetles, health nerds and classy highbrow types – it's for everyone. Even scallywags like me.

And that's how my ridiculous healthy food blog, *Shannon's Kitchen*, was born.

I don't believe there's one particular way everyone should eat because everybody is different. While one bloke is pumping on a vegan diet, some other poor chick tries it and ends up so anaemic she'd be willing to suck a scabby, bleeding dick just for the goddamn iron. One woman swears by the paleo 'lifestyle' but another gives it a go and ends up having to wee out a kidney stone that leaves her urethra in tatters. One bloke is all about the ketogenic diet; another tries it, faints on the bus and does a wee in his trousers. We're all different.

This cookbook is silly as fuck. I mention doodles and nipple boners far too much but the recipes are achievable, tasty and will give you food you'll actually fucking eat.

Hope you enjoy it,

SHANNON x

RATINGS
HOW MANY FUCKS WILL I NEED TO GIVE AND HOW TASTY IS IT?

Allow me to introduce you to my patented* Recipe Rating Systems:

HOW MANY FUCKS WILL I NEED TO GIVE?

Before we consider cooking a meal, we all want to know: 'How many fucks will I need to give?' Sometimes you have all the fucks to give, and sometimes you would rather punch yourself in the genitals to excuse yourself from fuck-giving. To make it easy for you, I have included a fuck-giving rating system. From this you can see if a meal will be a piece of piss or if it will require more of a fuck-giving investment.

1. **This is some easy shit.**
2. **This requires moderate fuck-giving.**
3. **You're going to need to saddle up a stiffie because the fucking-giving odds are high.**

HOW TASTY IS THIS SHIT?

Sometimes you're happy to just slap some nourishing shit together and call it a day. Other days your tongue is hankering for a good time. To make it easy, I have developed a nipple erection rating system. Just how sprightly will my nipples become on tasting this dish? Are we talking a little tingle in Leftie? Or is this so tasty I'm going to be sporting a serious set of raging nipple boners?

1. **Pretty tasty.**
2. **Very fucking tasty.**
3. **So damn tasty you've sprouted a third nipple because two nipp-stiffies isn't enough to express the excitement.**

* Not actually patented because as if I know how to fucking patent stuff.

WHAT THE FUCK IS THIS FOOD ABOUT?

If you are like me, then you give moderate fucks about your health. You're not a frequent flyer with Ronald the Questionable Clown; no, you have your shit more together than that. But you're not such an uptight flog that you're activating your nuts and adding fucking bee pollen to your smoothies. No way. If you're paying $20 for a tiny packet of powder, it's sure as fuck not bee pollen. You're just a sensible legend trying to look after yourself and lead a bloody good and fun life. The food in this cookbook is here to support that. I don't believe in superfoods, organic shit, detoxes or diets – just basic, healthy, tasty shit. I'm not promising that you'll become so hot that you'll have to carry a baton to club away unsolicited erectile tissue pointing in your direction. And I'm not promising that you'll become a skinny bitch because, who gives a fuck? This is about health, not hotness. Here is what the food in this cookbook is all about:

Lots of fucking vegetables. Because they are just so fucking good for you. This is the one thing that health professionals, health nerds and internet psychos can agree on – eat your fucking vegetables. Everyone agrees: from the doctor in the white coat, to the bikini-clad babe drinking from a coconut, to the expert dietician, to the whimsical health-nut with the dreamcatcher necklace. The benefits of eating vegetables are endless. You should aim for at least 5 serves a day. So let's make those fuckers tasty and get it done.

Not a shitload of added sugar. We've all received the very sad memo that sugar is a bit of a fuckstick. It'd be awesome if researchers would discover that sugar is not such a doodlebug after all, and we could welcome it back into society with open arms. I would love nothing more than to pop open a celebratory bag of Skittles. But it's looking unlikely. The vast majority of modern research suggests excessive sugar is a bit of a menace. You can still have some but just take it fucking easy.

Get some nuts into you. Unless you're allergic, in which case, don't: that would be very silly. But most non-allergic people don't eat enough nuts. Like other plant foods, they are nutritional legends: they have great fats, vitamins, minerals, protein and offer sustained energy. Plus, in the flavour department, they are total nipple erection material.

Eat a variety. You might notice there's fuck all wheat in this book, and it's not to encourage you to cut wheat out, it's to encourage you to add other shit in (like other grains, nuts or vegetables). Sorry to be a fucklord but I'm just thinking of your bowels. We should be eating lots of different plants. Variety is important – which is why I may sign Mr Shannon and I up for a swingers club when we get bored of each other's privates.

Enjoy your fucking food. This life isn't a test run. This is the big one, it's not a reccy, so enjoy it for fuck's sake. Eat delicious food but don't eat too much shit or you might end up inadvertently clipping a few years off. Alive: good. Dead: not so good. But existing on protein shakes and salads? I would rather be dead.

ANYTHING WEIRD I MIGHT NEED?

I'm clearly not a flash fuck, so expect all ingredients to be available at a regular supermarket (I mean, probably not some shitty little supermarket that also doubles as the local post office and lottery agency). Here are some things I always have in my kitchen and you'll see them frequently used in this cookbook.

WEIRD-ARSE FLOURS

'Shannon, why don't you just use normal fucking wheat flour and stop being such a goddamn penis?!' Well, we get enough wheat in our lives so branching out and adding something different or more nutritious is just bloody sensible.

Almond meal. It works a fucking treat in cakes. You MUST keep this sealed up and use it quickly. It goes off pretty fast and ruins cakes and lives. But when it's fresh it is so tasty and makes super moist cakes. It's healthy because it is made from fucking almonds, obviously.

Coconut flour. This guy has a fair amount of protein and fat, and is lighter on carbohydrates. We use this in small amounts because it can be as dry as all fuck.

Tapioca flour. Another grain-free alternative which is made from the roots of cassava plants. Sounds wanky as fuck but give it a go.

FATS AND OILS

Bring us the flavour, fats.

Butter. Margarine is a sick joke. It masquerades as a health food and tastes like a dildo – just don't do it to yourself. Butter wins.

Coconut oil. I'm not being a silly sausage and trying to tell you this is a miracle food because it fucking isn't. But it is a very tasty oil with some good features and it's good in cakes, slices, stir-fries and curries. NOT A FUCKING SUPERFOOD THOUGH.

A variety of oils. I use a selection including olive, macadamia, sesame, peanut and duck fat.

SWEET SHIT

These are alternatives to refined sugars. This shit is STILL SUGAR, there's no skirting around that. So why fucking bother? I do because it's generally less processed, has a lower glycemic index (meaning slower release of sugars), has some minerals (although very fucking little in the grand scheme of things) and for me it's also about taste. Where we can we'll use fruits (like bananas, apples or dates), but sometimes you just have to pull out the fucking hard stuff like maple syrup and honey.

RANDOM SHIT YOU'LL NOTICE I USE A FAIR BIT

Apple cider vinegar. FLOG ALERT.

Balsamic vinegar. I use this shit heaps to add flavour.

Cacao powder. This is basically the raw version of cocoa (a more nutritious version). It's got a gorgeously strong chocolate flavour. It's usually in the health food aisle of the supermarket. If this fucks you off, then go ahead and use regular unsweetened cocoa.

Chia seeds. These little seeds are full of omega-3 fatty acids, which are very fucking good for you. They also pack fibre for your arse-pipe. You'll find them in the health food aisle of the supermarket.

Coconut milk. I just fucking like it. I don't consume heaps of dairy, it doesn't particularly agree with my inners (it makes my inners want to join my outers). Other than good iron levels, coconut milk doesn't have that much to offer you so feel free to swap it out for regular cow's milk or whatever tickles your fancy.

Fresh herbs/roots. You just have to embrace fresh chilli, ginger and garlic, there's no dodging this. You'll just make an arsehole out of yourself if you use the jarred stuff. But feel free to be a short-cutting arsehole if you need to, we aren't awarded infinite fucks to give in life.

Fresh Medjool dates. 'Because your arsehole is worth it.' These little guys are full of vitamins and minerals, and they help you shit – they even look like tiny little poos. How delightful. You'll find these in the fresh fruit section. They are sugary as fuck and super tasty, which is why I use them in cakes and treats.

Kewpie mayonnaise. Is this a health food? Haha. No. But who the fuck cares. It is a beyond delicious Japanese mayonnaise. Here in Australia the supermarkets seem to be a bit racist and put this in the 'Asian Section'. 'Straya will let the Asian foods in but they have to keep to their own sections.

Kitchen gear. Look, I'm sorry but you kind of need a food processor for many of these recipes (or at least a decent blender). I'll admit they're expensive as fuck, and harder to clean than Charlie Sheen's crotch, but they're worth it.

Nuts. Fucking heaps of them. Nuts are very bloody good for you – except for the poor Milhouses who are allergic to them. Nut allergies are very fucking serious and must be respected, so please don't pack any nutty food in kids' lunchboxes, it's just an arsehole move.

Peanut butter. Because PEANUT FUCKING BUTTER. Choose one with only two ingredients: peanuts and a bee's dick of salt. I'm not sure peanut butter is officially a health food but I'm going to completely fucking ignore that factoid.

Spices. I am a spice bandit so prepare to have cumin, garam masala, smoked paprika, ground coriander, cinnamon, nutmeg and more at the ready.

Sriracha sauce. Australian supermarkets are inconsistent with their racism and put this with the other sauces instead of shepherding it into the Asian Section. This is the best chilli sauce ever. I use it HEAPS. It has some sugar but it's worth it and anyone who argues will have it squirted in their eyes.

Tahini. This is toasted sesame seeds whipped up, and you'll find it in the health food aisle. It has heaps of calcium and is tasty as fuck.

Tamari. This is a fermented soy sauce. Soy and tamari taste pretty friggin' similar except tamari is thicker and less salty (and often gluten-free).

BREAKFAST SHIT

GROWING PANCAKES

I'm one of those cruel parents who serves their children imitation junk food. I know – there is a special place in the bowels of hell reserved for sneaky fucks like me. But as my oldest son is growing up, I am introducing him to the notion of growing food versus fun food. Growing food helps you grow strong. Fun food is . . . well . . . fucking fun. He knows there's nothing wrong with eating a bit of fun food, as long as you're balancing it out with enough growing food. He experienced the consequences of overdoing it firsthand at one of his little chum's birthday parties. There was a Peppa Pig cake, fairy bread, lollies, sausages, chips, and a token fruit platter which no child gave a single fuck about. I let him go balls deep. He got his trotters into all of it (except the bloody fruit platter). He was loving it, he was pinging. Until he wasn't. The poor possum got the guts-ache of his life and spewed like his daddy did at his buck's night (except his face wasn't covered in whipped cream and mystery pussy-juice). He now understands the concept of dietary balance. MOTHER OF THE YEAR. This imitation junk food recipe is a winner – my kid actually prefers Growing Pancakes over the regular ones, what a little dork. But in his defence, they are so bloody tasty.

DO IT

1 Get your blender or food processor out.

2 Plonk all the wet ingredients in and whizz that shit – eggs, milk, vanilla, coconut oil, maple syrup.

3 Now add the dry bits (almond meal, flour, baking powder, salt) and whizz the absolute fuck out of it. I'm talking a full minute or so.

4 Get a frypan heating up over medium heat and grease that pan with butter because life is short and pancakes deserve butter.

5 Pour the batter in. You can make big'ns or small'ns. Just know that, like a heavy rooting partner, big ones are hard to flip.

6 These pancakes can burn easily because of the almond meal, so keep an eye on the cheeky flogs. They will make an arsehole out of you if you give them half an opportunity. They'll need flipping in 1–2 minutes. The other side will cook pretty quick so just watch and be on the ball.

7 When they're cooked you can eat them nude or serve them however you would normal pancakes. Put fucking ice cream on them if you want. I'm not watching . . . Or am I?

Serves 2–3

3 eggs

¼ cup (60 ml) milk of your choice (coconut, cow, almond or whatever the fuck you like)

1 teaspoon vanilla extract

1 tablespoon coconut oil

2 tablespoons maple syrup

1 cup (120 g) almond meal

¼ cup (35 g) self-raising flour (regular or gluten-free)

1 teaspoon baking powder

¼ teaspoon salt

Butter to fry those tasty fuckers in

HONEY & NUT BARS

I used to be a morning person. An early riser? Haha, fuck no, but I was fairly cheerful and functional on waking. As a child it meant creeping out of a cosy bed to feed and cuddle my pony, Finn. That little porker didn't like being made to wait for his chaff and hay, and I didn't make him, not when he paid in muzzle-kisses. I managed to retain my morning vigour as a young nurse, even when shiftwork required showing up at work in a civilised state at 7am. Despite the early rise, I could care for my patients without wanting to clamp their catheter, poke their sore wounds or administer punitive needles to faces. Now, after welcoming two small children, in the morning I am shouting at the sun, 'Why must you continue to rise, you shining ball of shit!' I'm tired. I'm not ready to get out of bed. BUT! When I remember that there are Honey & Nut Bars waiting for me in the fridge, all of a sudden it's not all doom and gloom, and I no longer wish for the heart of our solar system's untimely demise. These are so fucking easy and such a treat.

DO IT

1 Pop the peanut butter and honey in a saucepan and melt over a low heat, then add in the salt and vanilla extract.

2 While it's all warm and runny, stir in the puffed rice. Make sure you do this while the mixture is still warm, otherwise it will be like trying to stir corn through shit.

3 Grease a slice tin (about 20 cm square) and line it with baking paper, then press the mixture in nice and flat. Whack it in the fridge for an hour, then it'll be safe to pull out and slice into bars.

4 Keep the bars in the fridge and prepare for them to be eaten fast as fuck.

Makes 12 bars

1 cup (280 g) peanut butter

4 tablespoons (115 g) honey

2 teaspoons vanilla extract

A bee's dick of salt

2½ cups (50 g) puffed rice (you'll find this in the health food aisle of the supermarket)

PUMPKIN BREAKFAST SCONES

FUCKS GIVEN

TASTINESS

Let me tell you the beautiful story of how I met my mother-in-law. It was a warm summer morning back in my and Mr Shannon's hometown of Yarrawonga. The magpies were outside, cackling their wonky, pretty call. Light was creeping in through the blinds, and I was curled up in bed with Mr Shannon, nude, calm, snuggly. And then BOOM. His mother walked in unannounced, yacking about breakfast, spotted me, said 'Shit!' and spun around like a rodeo bronco and got the fuck out of there. That wasn't how I was hoping it would go. I was hoping to have my titties covered at the very least and I was definitely hoping there wouldn't be an unexplained bottle of olive oil right beside me. But anyway, we joined her at her breakfast table and, as I sat there in her son's t-shirt, she probably thought I was a total jizzbucket but she didn't let on and she still hasn't. I love her. These Pumpkin Scones are a delicious breakfast, but they require some fucks to be given, so you probably wouldn't pull them out for some unexpected rootrat.

DO IT

1 Heat the oven to 190°C (fan-forced) and line a baking tray with baking paper.

2 Mix all your wet ingredients together in a bowl (pumpkin, eggs, vanilla essence, maple syrup) and set it aside for later. Get your food processor out and plonk in the almond meal, coconut flour, tapioca flour, salt, baking powder, cinnamon and nutmeg. Give it a little whizz until it is combined.

3 Now pop the cold chunks of butter in and pulse it until it looks crumbly.

4 It's time for all that wet shit to join the party: pour it into the food processor. Keep blitzing this until it all sticks together. Don't overdo it. When it looks smooth, just leave it the fuck alone. You'll need to let it sit there for about 15 minutes to firm up, otherwise it's way too bloody gooey.

5 Now we are making the little scones. You can't roll this out like normal scones, it's too bloody sticky. So I use my hands to ball up little scones (I put gloves on like a little friggin' princess). Make the scones about 5 cm across and 2 cm high.

6 Place them on the baking tray and cook for about 12 minutes (could be anywhere from 9–15 minutes depending on how big those little fucks are and your oven's intensity), look for them turning golden brown, slightly more so on the edges. When you get them out of the oven, they honestly look like shit-rocks of doom. You'll think, 'Fuck you, Shannon'. But despair not – they are tasty little nuggets.

7 When they're out of the oven, pop them straight on a cooling rack for about 10 minutes.

8 Serve them up warm, slice them in half and smother them with fucking butter.

Makes about 10

½ cup (200 g) cooked pumpkin, mashed well, cooled

2 eggs

1 teaspoon vanilla essence

¼ cup (60 ml) maple syrup

1 cup (120 g) almond meal

½ cup (75 g) coconut flour

½ cup (75 g) tapioca flour

¼ teaspoon salt

1 teaspoon baking powder

2 teaspoons cinnamon

1 teaspoon nutmeg

⅓ cup (75 g) butter, cold and cubed

TO SERVE

A fuck-tonne of butter*

*If you don't like butter, then just keep on walkin' because these sons of bitches are nothing without butter on top.

BREAKFAST TART

Well, well, well, single serve breakfast-dessert. 'Calling all cat ladies!' Just fucking with you, I give full respect to single cat ladies. They know where it's at. While they may not have D/whistle/pizzle/spatchcock/skin-flute/winkie/100%-all-beef-thermometer/beaver-basher/dangler/tromboner/piss-weasel/dingaling/meat-popsicle/disco-stick/cum-gun/peepee/spawn-hammer/man-rocket/pant-serpent/hot-rod/todger/flesh-torpedo/wang/pink-joystick on tap, they are independent as fuck and can do what they want, when they want. Just so long as that does not involve patting the bellies of their cats without explicit invitation, waiting too long to feed their cats, or unwillingness to let cats inside, then back outside, then straight back inside again. Cats will not stand for that sort of selfishness, because they are total douche-canoes. Mr Shannon has curbed my cat levels firmly at one because my old kitty is, quite frankly, a fucking jerk and continues to hiss at him randomly after 8 years of knowing him. God I love her. Anyway, this brekkie is a ripper, it's a treat of a way to start the day.

DO IT

1 Grease a little 10 cm'ish ramekin.

2 Make The Base Bit first by chucking all the ingredients into a food processor and whizz the fuck out of it until it looks crumbly and sticky.

3 Press it into the base of the ramekin and put it in the fridge to harden up. Like every doodle does when it sees me. Just kidding, I'm actually very mediocre with low stiffie-induction ratios.

4 Now make The Stuff. Just put the yoghurt, honey, chia seeds, vanilla and raspberries in the food processor and whizzle-dizzle it until it looks smooth. The raspberry seeds will be throughout it all but that will mask the shitty little chia seeds which is grouse.

5 Spoon The Stuff onto the base and then return it to the fridge to have an overnight chill session.

6 When morning comes prepare yourself by sticky-taping your penis/clitoris down because this tart is fucking delicious and spontaneous erections may occur without warning.

Serves 1

THE BASE BIT

5 Medjool dates, pitted

2 teaspoons coconut oil (or soft butter)

⅓ cup (45 g) macadamias
(or cashews or almonds), roasted

¼ cup (20 g) desiccated coconut

THE STUFF IN THE TART

½ cup (140 g) yoghurt (I like coconut yoghurt but natural yoghurt is fly as fuck too)

1 teaspoon honey (or maple syrup)

1 teaspoon chia seeds (if you want a firmer tart, use 2 teaspoons, but I like it kind of soft)

½ teaspoon vanilla extract

12 raspberries

TO SERVE

How about a cheeky bit of extra yoghurt and raspberries?

MANGO MOUSSE

Everybody has funny little quirks and aversions. I have a deep distaste for pubes. When they are attached, I can tolerate them. Don't get me wrong, I don't enjoy them, but we can coexist. The second they become detached I am like, 'No, fuck this shit'. If they are laying on the bathroom floor I step over them like curly little land mines. It's brutal. Unfortunately, Mr Shannon drops them like confetti at a Mardi Gras, so it is a constant battle. Mr Shannon's ridiculous aversion is to fruit. Yes, fruit. What a flog. He makes this squinty little face like every piece of fruit in the history of the world is a fucking lemon. His lips purse up in revulsion and his eyes wince like they're about to be poked. We call it 'fruit face'. It's highly annoying, but I care about that doodlebug and I want him to eat some damn healthy fruit. So I make him shit like this Mango Mousse. It is creamy, nutritious and zero fruit face to be seen.

DO IT

1 Soak the chia seeds in the milk. Give it about 30 minutes to get a bit sticky and gelatinous.

2 Now get your friend, The Blender. Bang the soaked chia seeds (and its milky, jizzy goo), mango, kiwi, dates and vanilla in and give it a razzin'.

3 Now divide that between two little bowls, top with sliced banana, and then whack a couple of spoonfuls of yoghurt on top.

4 Pop it in the fridge overnight.

5 In the morning, to bring the crunch, sprinkle the macadamias on top.

Serves 2

1 tablespoon white chia seeds (the dark chia seeds are fine but make it look like poo)

½ cup (125 ml) coconut milk (or normal milk, or water)

1 cup (200 g) mango, diced (I often use the frozen stuff, thawed)

2 fresh kiwifruits, peeled

5 Medjool dates, pitted

1 teaspoon vanilla extract

1 banana, sliced

Coconut yoghurt (or plain yoghurt), to serve

Little handful of macadamias (or some other tasty nut), roasted and chopped

STEWED PRUNE CHIA POTS

Have you ever had to contemplate taking a poo out a car window? I have. Some years back, Mr Shannon and I visited Africa. Part of our trip saw us driving ourselves. We had rented a car and, like the pair of dicks we are, we ended up with a vehicle completely fucking inappropriate for the task. It was ludicrously small and looked as though its wheels where sticky-taped on. Night fell and we were trying to find our way to accommodation in a reserve. The track started out wide, and got progressively smaller and more twisted, and the grass alongside grew taller and thicker, until the track was just two little tyre marks amongst the tall growth. We became lost. In Africa. In the equivalent of a bloody Hyundai Excel. 'We're fucking lost! Let's turn around and go back!' I said. 'Ahhh, how? We can't exactly pull a U-ey,' Mr Shannon sagely advised. 'Let's just reverse out!' I suggested. 'The car would barely make it out going forwards. Don't worry, we have two bottles of wine! We can just stay in the car tonight,' Mr Shannon said. 'What if we need a wee?! Wild Africa means lions, leopards and other cute but deadly fuckers that might want to eat you.' 'Don't worry! I can stick my dick out the window and wee!' . . . 'What about me?!' 'You'll just have to be quick or piss in an empty wine bottle.' My aim ain't that good so this was one occasion I was desperate to stall all bodily functions. Imagine if I'd eaten a Stewed Prune Chia Pot beforehand – I would have also had to become very creative with life-preserving car-defecation, and I'm not sure a marriage can survive that.

DO IT

1 Get your prunes stewin'. Just put them in a small saucepan with the water and vanilla and cook over a high heat until it bubbles, then turn it back to a simmer. Leave it to cook till it's super soft (about 20–30 minutes) and most of the water has evaporated.

2 Make the chia pudding by mixing the chia seeds, milk, vanilla and cinnamon together. That's seriously fucking it.

3 Divide the chia mixture between two little pots or bowls, then spoon the prune compote over the top or stir it through.

4 Whack it in the fridge. Like an ageing penis, you need to allow plenty of time for the pudding to firm up.

5 Come morning time, place some bandaids over your teats because you may sport some nipple erections on tasting this simple but lovely breakfast, and we wouldn't want to start the day with a case of chafe. These pots are ugly as fuck but taste lovely.

Serves 2

THE PRUNE PART

20 or so prunes

½ teaspoon vanilla extract

1 cup of water

THE CHIA PART

2 tablespoons chia seeds

1 cup milk of your choice (I like coconut milk)

½ teaspoon vanilla extract

Sprinkle of cinnamon

TO SERVE

I just eat this nude, but feel free to pull a cheeky one and whack some peanut butter and banana on this motherfucker in the morning

RASPBERRY BREAKFAST CAKE

This cake has four eggs in it so we can tell ourselves that it qualifies as a reasonable option for breakfast. Even if it doesn't, fuck it, I really don't give a shit. I could tell you about the protein, and the good fats and the god damn fruit, but do I really need to say anything other than 'cake for fucking breakfast'? Only a knob-jockey would question it. A slice of this nutritious fucker goes beautifully with a morning cuppa. My toddler wants to tell you that Raspberry Breakfast Cake also goes brilliantly with water served in a dinosaur cup, specifically with a curly straw. But that little unit happily ate several cat pellets and a ladybug sticker the other day so I'm not sure we can fully trust that adorable doodlehead's opinion.

DO IT

1 Preheat oven to 170°C (fan-forced).

2 Grease a loaf tin (25 cm x 13 cm) and line that fucker with baking paper so your brekkie cake will come out like a champ.

3 This cake is easy as fuck to make, and the easiest way is with a food processor (but it can be done with hand beaters or a whisk if you want to build up your guns). Combine all the wet bits (eggs, milk, coconut oil, maple syrup, vanilla extract) and whizz it for half a minute.

4 Now add in the almond meal, coconut flour, salt and baking powder and whizz all this until it's all consistent. It'll look a bit thick but don't stress, the cake won't turn out as dry as an old penis.

5 Now it's time to stir in the frozen raspberries. Don't be a fucking rough nut – be tender so they don't get smooshed.

6 Spoon the batter into the tin and smooth the top (it's thick as shit). Bake for about 45 minutes or until golden brown on the top and the sides are pulling away from the tin (like a hot chick away from an ugmo-creep on the dance floor).

7 Leave the cake in the tin for about 5 minutes, then turn it out and let it cool its tits on a rack. Best eaten fresh and warm, just like one's loin-chops.

Serves 8

4 eggs

½ cup (125 ml) milk (cow, coconut, almond or whatever you like)

¼ cup (60 ml) coconut oil

⅓ cup (80 ml) maple syrup

1 teaspoon vanilla extract

1 ½ cup cups (180 g) almond meal

½ cup (75 g) coconut flour

¼ teaspoon salt

2 teaspoons baking powder

1 cup frozen raspberries
(generally cheaper and available all year, and work better than fresh)

GO-TO GREEN SMOOTHIE

I didn't want to include any smoothies in this cookbook because they're just so tossbaggish and I wanted to keep the health-knob factor fairly minimal. But I actually drink this smoothie a-fucking-lot. It's quick and easy, and means I have started the day with a couple of serves of vegetables and fruit under my belt, meaning I can strut around smug as fuck in my yoga pants. I'm fucking with you. I don't wear yoga pants. From the front it would look as though I was smuggling a Double Stuffed Oreo in there and I don't even want to imagine what the rear view would be like, but I suspect it wouldn't be dissimilar to some sort of draught horse or heavy vehicle. This smoothie is pretty tasty, and your organs will just fucking love this healthy shit.

DO IT

1 Just whack all of that shit in a blender and whizz the bejesus out of it.

2 Pour it in a cup, and drink it with a straw. For some weird fucking reason it just tastes better with a straw. Planet-loving-plastic-haters can use reusable ones like I do. But for the love of god, rinse that straw straight after – if the smoothie dries inside it's harder to clean than a fanny that has been penetrated by Hugh Hefner. I reckon that ol' sausage has seen the inside of more than a few unfresh clams and would probably require a bottle-brush chaser.

Serves 1

1 penis-sized cucumber
(a chubby one, not a limp one)

3 handfuls of baby spinach

½ an avocado

1 banana

1 cup (250 ml) of coconut water OR apple juice OR orange juice OR water (or a combination of these)

1 lemon, peeled, obviously

3–6 square cm of fresh ginger (I go large, but that might be too gingery for some buffoons)

GOOD MORNING APPLE CRUMBLE

Ahh, mornings. Some humans love them and some humans would like to punch the aforementioned morning-lovers in the neck. For those who don't pounce out of bed, mornings can be a bit of a bastard. Many would prefer to snooze/be an arsehole/play on their phone while shitting in the fortress of solitude than get up and make a healthy god damn breakfast. So this recipe is for them. You make it the night before when you're not in fuckface-mode. This brekkie is tasty as all buggery and will increase your fibre and omega-3 intake while simultaneously reducing your likelihood of inflicting larynx-punches/angry tooting the car in front for taking 0.7 of a second too long to respond to a green light/calling your co-worker a lazy cunt. You're welcome, you grumpy fucks.

DO IT

1 In a bowl combine the grated apple, oats, chia seeds, honey, coconut milk and cinnamon. Give all that shit a bit of a stir and cover it, then bang it in the fridge. That cheeky little brew will sit overnight and the oats will become creamy and soft.

2 Now it's Topper time. You can make this the night before or in the morning, depending on projected levels of morning arseholery. All you have to do is chop or crush the macadamias and mix those crushed little fuckers with the coconut and nutmeg.

3 Morning has broken, and so has your spirit. It's now the a.m. so sprinkle that crunchy shit on top and have yourself a good morning, fuckface.

Serves 1

THE BODY

1 apple, grated

⅓ cup (30 g) rolled oats

1 teaspoon chia seeds

1 teaspoon honey

⅛ teaspoon ground cinnamon (pre-fucking-cise)

⅔ cup (160 ml) coconut milk (or whatever milk)

THE CRUMBLE TOPPER

1 tablespoon desiccated coconut

Small handful of macadamias, roasted

Sprinkle of nutmeg

CARAMELLO BANANA PORRIDGE

Porridge doesn't have to be a bowl of gluggy shit. Although my childhood recollection of it is exactly that. When I was a young teen, I went to a camp designed for girls who were either troublesome or severely henpecked. Believe it or not, despite my current poor behaviour, at that time I was not from the troublesome category. I was a homely little nerd, a real dorkface. I had a set of teeth best suited to a small fucking horse, frizzy wild hair, spots, an obsession with animals, a distinct aversion to cool kids (and humans in general), and a taste for academic success. Oh yes, the boys were just lining up to cop a feel of this teenage dreamboat. At this camp, breakfast every day was porridge. It was sticky as all fuck because the only milk available had to be squeezed from Daisy's dangling teets by us little fools, and our cow-nipp handling skills were about as ace as our people skills (some of the troublesome girls were actually good milkers thanks to their wristy-giving experience). It took many years to be able to look porridge in the eye again but I'm bloody glad we reconciled because this easy Caramello Banana Porridge is just delicious.

DO IT

1 Put the oats, banana, dates, coconut milk and water in a small saucepan over a high heat until it starts bubbling, then turn the heat down low and let it simmer for 5–10 minutes (if you're a total microwave bandit, you can cook it in the microwave instead on high for 2–3 minutes, stirring at the halfway point.
For fuck's sake use a sensible vessel – you can't put a saucepan in the microwave unless you enjoy explosions and the life of a burns victim).

2 Pop the porridge into a bowl and then add milk of your choice to get the consistency you seek. If you're a total bad-arse like me, feel free to sprinkle on some cinnamon and drop a wad of peanut butter on top.

Serves 1

⅓ cup (30 g) rolled oats

1 banana, peeled and chopped

4 Medjool dates, pitted and chopped

½ cup (125 ml) coconut milk

½ cup (125 ml) water (and add more if it gets too thick during cooking)

TO SERVE – ENTIRELY OPTIONAL

Sprinkle of cinnamon

Extra milk if desired (I like coconut, you can have whatever the fuck you like)

Spoon or 7 of peanut butter

Honey, if you're keen

ROSEWATER BROWN RICE PUDDING

'Breakfast is the most important meal of the day!' exclaimed some dopey cunt a million years ago. Whatever, fuckwit, we don't have time to place importance on food preparation when we are too busy pulling boogers out of our eyes, mustering up the energy for a morning shit, and wondering how we're going to get through the workday without punching Darren from Accounts. This cheeky little number is a ripper because you can cook it beforehand and stow it away in the fridge for morning-time, when the sun has risen but your will to live is still hiding under the covers. This dish is delicious hot or cold and lets you start your day feeling a whole lot less stabby, which is great news for that fuckstick Darren. I fucking love this Rosewater Brown Rice Pudding, it's total breakfast-dessert.

DO IT

1 Pop the pears in a saucepan with the apple juice, vanilla, cinnamon and cardamom, and cook over a medium-high heat. Let them simmer until they are soft and lovely (about 30–40 minutes). Take the lid off halfway through.

2 While the pears are cooking, make the rice pudding. Bang the rice, water and salt into a saucepan and bring to the boil over a high heat. Then dial it down a notch so that it's just simmering away for about 5 minutes until it's looking a bit dry. Then add in a cup of coconut milk and the vanilla essence, and get it simmering again. Stir occasionally and every 10 minutes add in another cup of coconut milk (3 in total). When you add the last cup of coconut milk, also add the honey and rosewater.

3 Cook the rice for about 30–40 minutes, until the rice is softer than my ageing titties which now resemble empty Santa-sacks. The rice pudding should look creamy and slightly gooey.

4 This is delicious hot or cold. Serve the pears and pudding as a duo and enjoy the fuck out of it.

Serves about 6

THE PEARS BIT

6 sliced ripe pears (not soggy-arse ones, still firm please)

½ cup (125 ml) apple juice

1 teaspoon vanilla extract

½ teaspoon cinnamon

4 cardamom pods (give them a little squash before they go in)

THE RICE PUDDING BIT

1 cup (200 g) brown basmati rice

1 cup (250 ml) water

A bee's dick of salt

3 cups (750 ml) coconut milk (or you can use full fat cow milk)

1 teaspoon vanilla essence

⅓ cup (115 g) honey

½ teaspoon rosewater (if you can't find rosewater, then use rosewater essence which can be found at the supermarket near the vanilla essence)

PUMPKIN & APPLE BREAKFAST SOUP

Soup for breakfast? Shannon, you're a knob. Yes, I am a knob. But if fancy-pants health nerdburger flogs can serve 'Smoothie Bowls' for breakfast, I can serve the warm version: fucking soup. There are three reasons why this soup is a winning breakfast: 1) You can cross off a couple of serves of vegetables at the start of the day and feel superior to all non-vegetable consuming peasants (and have a donut for morning tea); 2) You can prepare it on the weekend, whack it into single serves and freeze them, so all you have to do in the morning is pull your dick and reheat the soup; 3) You can dip some buttery toast in that tasty shit. If I had a mic I would drop it.

DO IT

1 Preheat your oven to 180°C (fan-forced).

2 Place the coconut oil into a roasting tray and whack it in the oven for a couple of minutes to melt, then remove the tray and throw the pumpkin, sweet potato, capsicum, apple and onion in there. Toss them around so they all get greased up. Then sprinkle on some smoked paprika, cinnamon and nutmeg. The final piece of the roasting puzzle is to throw the rosemary on top as a whole sprig.

3 Roast them for 50–60 minutes until they're soft and have slightly charred edges.

4 Make the soup by chucking those veggies, the rosemary leaves, the stock and coconut milk into a blender/food processor and whizz the shit out of it until it's perfectly smooth. If it's too thick for your delicate palate, then add more stock.

5 Serve with a tiny sprinkle of nutmeg and a congratulatory nipple tweaking.

Serves a shitload

1 tablespoon coconut oil (or whatever oil or fat)

1 medium pumpkin, peeled and cut into chunks

1 sweet potato, peeled and cut into chunks

2 red capsicums, cut into strips

2 apples, cored and quartered

1 onion, peeled and quartered

Sprinkle of smoked paprika, cinnamon and nutmeg

1 dick-length sprig of fresh rosemary (a fired-up one, not a sleepy one)

2 cups (500 ml) lamb stock (or you can use chicken or veggie stock). If you like runnier soup then you'll need more than this

1 or 2 cups (250–500 ml) coconut milk (depends how you creamy you like it)

TO SERVE

Sprinkle of nutmeg

HALLOUMI FRITTERS

You know those people who wake up looking fresh and glamorous and full of life? I am not one of those people. I wake up looking deceased. In the morning I want to drink coffee, cuddle dogs and maybe do a shit. Specifically in that order. I don't want to have to deal with a poo first thing. Unless it's a clean and jerk (you know the ones where the second wipe is just to confirm that you weren't dreamin' when the first wipe came up clean? Yeah, you know the one). So no, come morning, I don't want to fuck around in the kitchen cooking a fancy breakfast. But sometimes you really want something hot and snazzy. These Halloumi Fritters are perfect because they don't require that you part with too many precious a.m. fucks, but they offer you a gorgeous, healthy cooked brekkie.

DO IT

1 Combine all ingredients (except the halloumi) in a mixing bowl.

2 Now we'll crunch up that halloumi: pop some oil in a large frypan over a medium heat. Add in the chopped halloumi and fry it until it's golden. You'll need to keep tossing it around.

3 Whack the fried halloumi in with the fritter mixture and stir through.

4 Heat up the frypan again over a medium heat. Whack in some more oil so the fritters don't stick like shit to a blanket. Scoop some mixture (a few tablespoons for each one) into the pan and fashion like little patties.

5 Cook them for about 3–4 minutes, flip them and cook a further 3 minutes, or until golden brown and cooked through.

6 Serve it up with some green shit so your bowels are happy and you feel good about yourself. Self esteem is fucking important.

Serves 2–4 depending what you're having with it

2 eggs, lightly beaten

1 tablespoon coconut flour

1 zucchini (about dildo size. Not a greedy dildo size, just a satisfactory ladylike size), grated

2 handfuls of finely chopped baby spinach

½ cup (80 g) corn kernels, steamed

2 spring onions, chopped

1 tablespoon Kewpie mayonaise

2 teaspoons Sriracha sauce

Salt and pepper

Oil for frying

100 g halloumi, diced into 1 cm square cubes

TO SERVE

How about some greens – like fresh baby spinach tossed in a smidgen of balsamic vinegar? And some avocado? Or live like a king and serve with smoked salmon or bacon

POACHED PEAR & BACON

Pear and bacon. 'Oh Shansie, you've clearly taken a bad pinger and suffered some sort of brain malfunction, because this is just silly business'. I have certainly experienced brain malfunctions before, but not from dodgy pingers, from child-related exhaustion. My second child, Herbie, often sleeps like a fuckwit. Since his arrival, I've been severely sleep deprived and operating with a decrepit, foggy noggin at times. One morning, after weeks of shit sleep, I left the kids with Mr Shannon while I grocery shopped. Alone. I took my time. God, it was total mum-luxury. My nipples are getting hard just thinking about it. I slowly zigzagged my way up the aisles, making considered decisions. Chubby baby Herbie wasn't shouting at me for bananas. Hyper vigilance wasn't required as old ladies' achilles were not in danger from my trolley-wielding preschooler, Jack. It was bliss. I got home late in the morning, relaxed and smiling. I was unpacking the shopping as I noticed a missed call on my phone. *Hmm, an international number. How odd.* I kept unpacking until finally, the penny fucking dropped. It was a call from a New Zealand radio station who had made an appointment to interview me over the phone. 'FUCK!' I shrieked. I ran in circles for a minute like a psycho hose-beast, then I calmed my tits and poured myself a glass of breakfast wine, skulled it, and quickly rang back and got to be cheeky on the radio. Herbie isn't such a ratbag sleeper these days and those malfunctions are hopefully behind me, so have no fear – this recipe is fucking on point.

DO IT

1 Get your pears going. Melt the butter over a low-medium heat in the frypan. Throw in the ginger and sage and give it a little stir. Place your pears into the frypan, with the lid on – they will take about 30 minutes to cook, with a few flips (if you want to expedite the fuck out of this, you can microwave the pears with a smidgen of water for about 2 minutes. Then they'll fry up in 5–10 minutes).

2 While the pears cook, get the bacon into a pan. Once it's done you just MUST fry up the baby spinach in the bacon fat because it is just stiffie material. The spinach will only take a minute to wilt and be perfect.

3 Serve up those gorgeous pears with the bacon, eggs of your choice and wilted spinach. A bit of goat's cheese or Persian feta goes fucking grouse with it, as does a cheeky sprinkle of dukkah if you can handle all that excitement.

Serves 2

THE PEARS BIT

2 pears, halved and cored

Decent knob of butter (teehee, knob)

1 teaspoon minced ginger

1 tablespoon fresh sage, finely chopped

THE REST

Bacon
I'm not going to say how much because bacon volume is a very sensitive topic and I'm not here to fucking judge

About 4 giant handfuls of baby spinach

Poached eggs (or however you like them)

TO SERVE – OPTIONAL

Sprinkle of dukkah

Goat's cheese or Persian feta

GREEN EGGS & HAM

Do you like green eggs and ham? Or do you say, 'No, fuck off, Shan!'
Eat them, cunt, they've got good shit, like protein and greens, you dopey tit,
Plus they're pretty easy to make, just chop some shit and give it a bake,
If it seems too much effort, you're wrong – it's a piece of piss, ya big ding-dong.

Maybe you don't like the green, but it'll give your rectum a lovely sheen!
Maybe you think, 'Eww, baked eggs! WHY?! That shit will be all festy and dry',
Heavens no, fuck that for a joke, there's a god damn runny yolk!
Prep time is nice and quick, so no need to be a fuckstick.

Will you cook them, sir or ma'am? Will you eat Green Eggs & Ham?
'It's bacon, not ham,' you madly say, 'What! Nah, yeah, alright, ok,
But it's bacon you crazy fuckstain, what sort of flog would complain?'
Go on, mate, give it a go, you'll fuckin' love it, I just know.

DO IT

1 Preheat the oven to 180ºC (fan-forced).

2 Heat some oil in a small ovenproof frypan, then fry your bacon until it's slightly crispy (or cooked to your liking).

3 Next add in the garlic, a sprinkle of cumin and the spinach. Give that a stir and let it wilt for a minute.

4 Now make a hole in the centre and crack in the eggs.

5 Place in the oven for 5–10 minutes (depending how firm you like the eggs).

6 While that's cooking, make the Saucey Sauce by mixing those ingredients together.

7 To serve, spoon the Saucey Sauce over the baked eggs.

Serves 1

2 rashers bacon, chopped

1 clove garlic, minced

Sprinkle cumin

3 handfuls of baby spinach, chopped

2 eggs

THE SAUCEY SAUCE

1 tablespoon natural yoghurt

½ teaspoon Sriracha sauce

Smidgen of lemon juice

Cracked pepper

TO SERVE

Optional – pine nuts

SALADY SHIT

THE BIG SALAD: BIGGER THAN ELAINE'S

This is the sort of meal that an arsehole's dreams are made of. I don't mean a figurative arsehole. I mean the literal exit point of poo from the rectum, what us highbrow types term 'the anus'. Ha! As if I'm highbrow. I don't think highbrow types have used a zucchini/petrol hose/5L wine bottle/syringe/Duplo tower/sunscreen bottle/catheter nozzle/pool noodle/hotdog/snowboard/wakeboard/kebab/various power tools/small mammal/fire hose as a makeshift phallus to accentuate and punctuate a humping motion (those fancy fucks are missing out). But anyway, yes, this recipe is for the anus. I probably can't sell it to you freshlords on the promise of a happy ring-piece alone – if we were committed to happy buttonholes we wouldn't wipe them so vigorously with goddamn paper. So let me tell you more. It's got nutrients aplenty – vitamins, minerals, antioxidants and all that shit. It's got crunch. It's got a fucktonne of green. Its dressing is delicious, because as usual in salad-land, without it this meal could go fuck itself. This is a big-arse salad, and you're going to like it. Elaine Benes would go crazy for this.

DO IT

1 Preheat the oven to 180°C (fan-forced).

2 Pop the cauliflower and pumpkin on a baking tray and drizzle some olive oil on top, then sprinkle the cumin and cinnamon over the top. Roast in the oven for 25–30 minutes.

3 While they're roasting, make the dressing by mixing the vinegar, mayo, mustard and honey together.

4 Whack the green shit, capsicum, quinoa and avocado in a salad bowl. Beforehand, I like to press my avocado's face into some shit (such as sesame seeds) to make it look fancy which makes the prospect of salad less suicide-provoking.

5 Throw the roasted cauliflower and pumpkin in there too.

6 Poach an egg (so the yolk is still runny, which takes 3–4 minutes) and plonk it on top. Then pour the dressing all over. If you've got shit to sprinkle on top (like dukkah, nuts or seeds), then drop it on.

7 Await the poo.

SERVES 1

THE SALADY SHIT

¼ head cauliflower, cut into florets

Handful of pumpkin, cut into small bite-size chunks

½ teaspoon cumin

¼ teaspoon cinnamon

Couple of handfuls of baby spinach and rocket, shredded

½ red capsicum, sliced

⅓ cup cooked quinoa (or brown rice)

½ an avocado, sliced

Poached egg (or cooked chicken)

Shit to sprinkle on top (I like dukkah or pine nuts or sesame seeds)

THE DRESSING

1 teaspoon rice wine vinegar

2 teaspoons Kewpie mayonnaise

2 teaspoons Dijon mustard

1 teaspoon honey

MANGO & LAMB SALAD

My cat really enjoys this dish. I know this because I once left my half-eaten salad on the table while I trotted upstairs to attend to a wakeful babe/pest. When I came back down, that furry arsehole was up to her whiskers in feta and mango. This indiscretion was added to her ever-growing list of sins: brazenly urinating on the stairs, relentlessly licking her buttonhole whilst laying on my bedspread (bizarrely loudly if I'm trying to go to sleep), continued and repeated undeserved hissings at Mr Shannon, cruel intimidation tactics used on the dogs, and backing out the stinkiest turd of all time in the car on a road trip. She's a real dickbeetle but her palate is on point. This salad is my go-to in summer because it is easier than a hoebag after last drinks have been called. Plus, as kitty knows, it's fucking tasty. Don't open yourself up to the heartache of using frozen mango though, it will only end in tears – you need freshies. So, when mango season arrives expect your salad intake to skyrocket, as mine does. My summer trolley has a large mango zone, only rivalled by the sanitary napkin zone I'm required to concurrently purchase to soak up all the inevitable Mango & Lamb Salad-related lady-area secretions.

DO IT

1 Whack the greens in a big-arse bowl. Chuck in the avocado, mango, lamb and feta.

2 Drizzle on the oil and the balsamic vinegar.

3 If you're having pine nuts, sprinkle them on top.

4 That's fucking it. How dare I even have the audacity to include this as a 'recipe'? Because I'm a dick but once you taste this you won't give a shit.

Serves 1

A few giant handfuls of baby spinach and rocket

½ an avocado, diced

½ to 1 mango, peeled and diced

Portion of cooked lamb, sliced.
I love using lamb cutlets or loin, cooked medium-rare because overcooked lamb is so tough you might as well be chewing on a severed finger you found in a discarded medical waste bin

1 or 2 tablespoons soft Persian feta, crumbled into little chunks

A smidgen of oil (I use the stuff the Persian feta is sitting in)

Balsamic vinegar to taste

Optional – ½ tablespoon of pine nuts if you can be fucked

GREEN CURRY SALAD

In the dead of night, I rolled over in bed and reached for Mr Shannon but he was missing. In his place lay a flat, carefully placed pillow case. 'How bizarre . . .' I thought. I went to lift the pillow case just as Mr Shannon reentered the room. 'Don't touch it!' he shouted. My hand quickly drew back. His face was white. It was pasty as fuck for two reasons: 1) shame and horror; 2) he was very fucking ill. After eating at some dodgy place in Thailand, the poor dear's bowels had been overcome by a raging bacterial plague and he had shit himself in his sleep. The fool had tried to protect me from his faecal onslaught with a flimsy pillowcase. I would like to tell you that was the one and only time that Mr Shannon explosively pooed within a one-metre radius of me but I would be lying. The dressing on this salad looks not dissimilar to what lay beneath that permanently desecrated pillowcase but that's where the similarities end. This is a tasty and healthy dish and poses no risk to your sheets or sleeping partner. As salads go, this Green Curry Salad is a fucking grouse one.

DO IT

1 Make the dressing first. Drain the peas and run them under cold water to cool their jets. Then whack them in a blender with the other dressing ingredients and whizz until it's smooth as fuck.

2 Make sure the cooked broccoli, zucchini and green beans are cool too, so run those green bastards under some cold water if they're not.

3 Divide the greenery and chicken between your bowls, then pour the dressing over the top.

4 Scatter the chopped nuts and coriander on top if you're jazzing it up like a fancy fuck.

Serves 2

THE DRESSING

½ cup (80 g) peas, cooked until soft

1 tablespoon green curry paste

½ cup (125 ml) coconut milk

1 tablespoon peanut oil

THE SALADY BIT

½ head broccoli, cut into florets, lightly steamed (5 minutes)

½ zucchini, cut into half moons, lightly steamed (5 minutes)

1 handful of green beans, lightly steamed (5 minutes)

Several handfuls of baby spinach and rocket, shredded

2 small portions cooked chicken, sliced

OPTIONAL

Small handful of fresh coriander, chopped

Small handful of cashews or peanuts, roasted and chopped

SEARED TUNA SALAD

Tuna salad. Sigh. Even I want to punch me in the fucking face. But this is actually very bloody tasty. This isn't skinny-bitch food, I mean, check out the amount of oil in this motherfucker. But it sure is nutritious. Omega-3 fatty acids are literally all over the place in this dish. Why would I give a shit about that? Because I have inherited my dad's high cholesterol and hardening of the arteries, meaning my heart is likely to shit itself one day. I also inherited his temper and nose. Yes, I have won the genetic lottery, thanks Dad. Now, let's get our fucking salad on.

DO IT

1 Make the dressing first by whacking all the ingredients in a bowl and whisking together.

2 Season the tuna with salt and pepper. Heat the sesame oil over a frypan on medium-high heat. Cook the tuna for 2 minutes each side (you can cook it longer if slightly rare fish freaks you out but you're doing yourself a giant fucking disservice and might as well use the tinned shit). Put the tuna aside and let it rest.

3 Place all the salad ingredients in a mixing bowl and toss them with the dressing. Divide between two plates or bowls. Now cut the tuna steaks into fine slices and place on top of the salad.

4 Crack a bit of pepper on top then crack yourself a celebratory stiffie – you've got yourself a delicious, healthy-as-fuck meal.

Serves 2

THE SALADY BIT

2 medium tuna steaks

1 tablespoon sesame oil

200 g green beans sliced diagonally, lightly steamed

3 eggs, medium-hard boiled, then peeled and quartered

1 small sweet potato, peeled, cubed and steamed

A few giant handfuls of baby spinach and rocket

200 g cherry tomatoes, halved

⅓ cup pitted black olives

THE DRESSING BIT

2 cloves garlic, minced

1 tablespoon Dijon mustard

1 tablespoon white wine vinegar

3 tablespoons olive oil

Salt and pepper

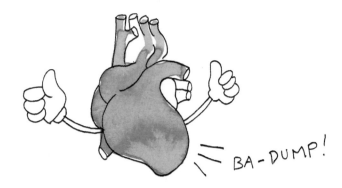

BA-DUMP!

PESTO CHICKEN SALAD

This is a ripper meal to prep on the weekend, divvy up and take to work for lunches. You might want to put a GPS tracker on the container though because if some fuckstick at work sees how strong your salad game is, they might try to pull a shifty one and swipe it. If your workplace is host to a fridge bandit but you don't have access to a tracking device, then you might want to consider putting a 'Stunt Pesto Chicken Salad' in the communal fridge. Make it look exquisite and irresistible but have the secret ingredient be a gargantuan portion of laxative. That will make it rather easy to finger the fridge bandit. As they head off to the toot, clutching their guts and clenching the fuck out of their sphincter so they don't publicly shit themselves, give them a cheeky wink as you pull the real Pesto Chicken Salad from an esky under your desk and bid them (and their jocks) good day. You can have this warm or cold, it's grouse either way.

DO IT

1 Preheat the oven to 200ºC (fan-forced).

2 Line a baking tray with baking paper. Plonk the broccoli and zucchini on one side of the tray, and place the chicken on the other half of the tray. Drizzle it all with olive oil and sprinkle some salt and pepper on.

3 Bake it in the oven for about 20 minutes, or until the veggies are slightly charred and the chicken is cooked through.

4 While that's happening, make the pesto. Get a food processor and add the pesto ingredients and pulse until a coarse pesto forms.

5 Get yourself a big fuck-off bowl and combine the roasted veggies, chicken, cherry tomatoes, spinach, rocket, walnuts and olives. Whack the pesto on top and toss it all to combine.

6 Serve it up and expect to prove Homer Simpson wrong – you CAN win friends with salad.

Serves 4

THE SALADY BIT

1 head broccoli, cut into florets

2 medium zucchini, sliced into half moons

500 g chicken breast, cut into bite-size chunks

2 tablespoons olive oil

Salt and pepper

1 cup (160 g) cherry tomatoes, halved

4 big handfuls of baby spinach and rocket

½ cup (60 g) walnuts, chopped

¼ cup (80 g) black olives, chopped

THE PESTO BIT

2 cups fresh basil

½ cup (40 g) parmesan cheese, roughly chopped

⅓ cup (50 g) macadamias, roasted

¼ cup (60 ml) olive oil

2 tablespoons lemon juice

2 cloves garlic

¼ teaspoon salt

PAD THAI SALAD

When I was a kid, salad pretty much consisted of iceberg lettuce, tomato and cucumber. Sometimes someone would try to be a flash fuck and put some salad onion, cheese or grapes in there. If you saw curly lettuce you were like, 'Wow. Where the fuck are we, The Ritz?!' Holy shit, hasn't salad come a bloody long way in a few decades? Despite this progression, most of the time I still feel like salad can go fuck itself. It's just so up itself and so righteously . . . salady. This one, however, can enter me without me recoiling in horror or feeling that I've boarded that decaying 'clean eating' bandwagon. It's a beauty. This recipe is pretty much as though pad thai and a regular salad had unprotected sexual relations, resulting in the most delicious inoffensive salad-baby ever.

DO IT

1 Make the dressing by combining all the Dressing Bits in a little bowl and stir.

2 Mix your chicken, cucumber, carrot, zucchini and spinach in a mixing bowl, pour the dressing over the top and toss it around.

3 Divide the salad between two plates, then sprinkle the coriander, mint and peanuts on top. That's friggin' it.

Serves 2

Cooked chicken, cut into little bite-size bits (I would say about 200 g but if you're greedier than that then so be it)

1 cucumber, peeled into strips that resemble noodles

1 carrot, peeled into strips

1 zucchini, peeled into strips

Epic handfuls of shredded baby spinach (or kale if you enjoy being a wankstain)

THE DRESSING BIT

1 clove garlic, super finely chopped

1 teaspoon rice wine vinegar

1 tablespoon honey

1 tablespoon peanut oil

1 teaspoon sesame oil

½ tablespoon fish sauce

1 teaspoon chilli flakes

TO SERVE

Coriander leaves, torn

Mint leaves, torn

Peanuts, crushed (about 2 tablespoons)

TOMATOEY FISH DISH

I was once foolish enough to partake in the phenomenon of 'Sail Croatia'. It involves sailing around the Adriatic Sea in a small vessel full of 20-odd young adults. It's pretty much party cruisin' with a high chance of procuring an STI and alcohol poisoning. It was quite fun. One day the sun rose on a particularly grim morning of the Hangover from Hell, but white water rafting was on the agenda so there was no hiding in the bunkbed. We were running very late, there was no time for breakfast or even a drink. And the thirst, my god, the THIRST. 'We'll get a drink when we get there', said Mr Shannon. But when we arrived, there were zero drinks. I looked around desperately for a tap but nothing. I strapped on a life-jacket and climbed aboard, thinking I would just drink from the river. But it wasn't a clear, fresh-looking thing, it was a murky-looking motherfucker. Hours passed and clear water never came. 'I could die in this yellow fucking boat', I thought. So I scooped up a mouthful of brown water and drank it. It could've been the unexplained foam, it could've been the visible dirt or it could have been the Jaeger bombs that evening but the next day I awoke wishing I hadn't. Croatia wasn't all doom and gloom though. After leaving the loveboat, Mr Shannon and I explored that gorgeous country and saw the clearest water we've ever seen at Plitvice Lakes (the sort of water you could drink without consequently shitting yourself). We ate beautiful fresh fish every single night – simple unpretentious dishes like this Tomatoey Fish Dish. This recipe might have an ingredients list that makes you want to punch my face but it's a piece of piss to make.

DO IT

1 Get a big-arse frypan over medium heat, splash in some olive oil, and then chuck in the onion and stir for a couple of minutes until it's slightly golden.

2 Add in the garlic, ginger, balsamic vinegar and honey, and fry that up for another couple of minutes – keep stirring, so it doesn't stick like a bastard.

3 Now add in the tomato paste, chopped tomatoes, Sriracha sauce (if using) and basil. Give that all a stir, then plonk in the capsicum and zucchini.

4 Let that cook for about 5 minutes, then add in the wine.

5 When that starts to simmer, place the fish fillets in and cook for 10–15 minutes (lid off), until cooked to your liking. You might need to turn them at the halfway point.

6 When it's cooked, sprinkle with the fresh parsley, and serve with mashed potato (or cauliflower puree if you're more of a health flog).

Serves 4

THE SAUCEY SAUCE

1 onion, finely chopped

2 cloves garlic, minced

3 square cm ginger, minced

1 tablespoon balsamic vinegar

2 teaspoons honey

2 tablespoons tomato paste

1 x 400 g tin chopped tomatoes

1 teaspoon Sriracha sauce (optional)

1 teaspoon dried basil

1 red capsicum, chopped

1 zucchini, chopped

½ cup (125 ml) white wine

Salt and pepper to taste

OTHER BITS

4 fillets of thick white fish

Handful of fresh parsley, chopped

Olive oil

TO SERVE

Mashed potato or cauliflower puree

FISH'N'CHIPS

What is a bogan? I'm not fully sure, the interpretation varies so wildly. Is it a champion embodying Australian working class culture? Is it an uncouth/unsophisticated person? An individual with a lack of pretence? If so, then sign me up, I'm fucking boges as. I'm unrefined and I don't give a shit. I wear tracksuit pants frequently, sometimes I don't wash my hair for a week, I burp entire sentences and my idea of theatre is taking the kids to see The Wiggles. Definitions aside, larrikinism and a lack of excessive fuck-giving are a big part of Australian culture. And so is fish'n'bloody-chips. I live by the beach so embracing fish'n'chips is pretty much mandatory down here. Here's a cheeky version you can do in your oven, so your poor little bowel doesn't get too chocked-full of refried grease. Sporting a greasy back nine is just too risky – you never know who might take advantage of it. I like to keep my ring-piece/ freckle/shit-winker in a state that can only be accessed with dogged perseverance and a shoehorn. Safety first.

DO IT

1 Heat your oven to 200°C (fan-forced).

2 Place your potatoes in a saucepan, cover with water and get those fuckers boiling. Boil them for about 15 minutes, until they're just slightly soft, then drain them and return them back into the saucepan over low heat to dry off for a minute or so.

3 Pour oil into a mixing bowl, and throw the potatoes in there. Toss them around so they're all covered in that filthy grease, like they're tiny little potato dicks about to be rammed up a poo-chute – you want those fuckers glistening. Now sprinkle the tapioca flour on top and re-toss.

4 Place the coated potatoes on a baking tray (line it with baking paper or grease the fuck out of it).

5 Now whack them in the oven and bake for 20–30 minutes, flipping every 10 minutes. Keep an eye on them so they don't burn and make an arsehole out of you. You'll know your chips are done when they have a gorgeous golden hue and looking at them makes your privates go all tingly.

6 While the chips are cooking, place your fish in an ovenproof dish, squeeze on the lemon and shake some salt and pepper on top. Pop the lid on and whack it in the oven with the chips. Cooking time varies on the size and type of fish, so you'll just have to work that out your damn self (15 minutes is a good ballpark – it's cooked when the fish is opaque).

7 Serve the fish nestled amongst the salad (YES, eat some bloody salad), and make sure you drop a load of salt on your chips like a fucking dump-truck.

Serves 2

THE FISHY BIT

2 fillets of fresh fish (whatever you fancy)

A squeeze of lemon juice

Salt'n'pepper

THE CHIPPY BIT

4 small potatoes, peeled and cut into chubby chips (make them about finger size. I'm talkin' chubby fingers, not scrawny little pokey ones)

Fuckloads of oil (melted duck fat is brilliant or olive oil – about ⅓ cup)

1 tablespoon tapioca flour

Salt, for the love of God, lots of salt

TO SERVE

Some fucking salad, ok?

MISO SALMON WRAPS

I've only been to Japan once but I loved it. Mr Shannon has been there quite a bit for snowboarding adventures. On one such trip with the lads, they took a shine to daily 'onsens' (where people get nude and bathe communally in hot springs). Apparently after a long day of boarding the slopes, there's nothing like getting your penis out with your friends. There was an evening where they had enjoyed a beer or 27 and were on the way home when one legend decided it was a good time for a cheeky dip. Except the poor fucker had mistaken a communal *cooking* onsen for a bathing one. It was 90 degrees Celsius. Of course, like many gentlemen, his body cannot support a fully operational brain because it primarily services the penile region and it wasn't until the next day he realised he had suffered very serious burns and required a trip to the hospital. I love that guy though, he's a ripper. And so are these tasty wraps which take inspiration from Japanese flavours. Healthy, easy, tasty as fuck. Enjoy.

DO IT

1 Mix together the miso paste, honey, rice wine vinegar and sesame oil. Then place the salmon fillets in it to marinate. If you have time leave it for an hour or so.

2 Make your wraps: get a frypan heating over a high heat. You need it fucking hot. While that's heating, make the batter by simply whisking the four ingredients together.

3 Pop oil in the super-hot frypan, then pour in half of the batter to make a big round wrap. After a few minutes, flip it over and cook the other side for a few minutes. You want it to be golden brown with a few charred bits. When it's done, place it on a cake rack to cool, and cook your next wrap. When they're both done, just leave them on the rack to cool.

4 Turn the frypan down to medium heat. Add in a little bit of oil. Then place your salmon in there. Place the lid on the frypan, and allow it to cook for 8–10 minutes, flipping it at the halfway point.

5 To serve, pop some avocado, greens and mayo into your wrap, then flake the salmon over the top. Roll it up and BOOM GOES THE DYNAMITE. You'll love it.

Serves 2

THE FISHY BIT

1 tablespoon miso paste

1 tablespoon honey

1 teaspoon rice wine vinegar

1 tablespoon sesame oil

2 small portions of salmon fillet (skinless)

Oil for cooking (I use peanut or coconut)

THE WRAP BIT

¾ cup (110 g) tapioca flour

¼ cup (35 g) coconut flour

1 cup (250 ml) water

1 egg

Oil for cooking (I use peanut or coconut)

TO SERVE

Avocado, sliced

Greens of your choice
(I like baby spinach and rocket)

Cheeky squeeze of Kewpie mayonnaise

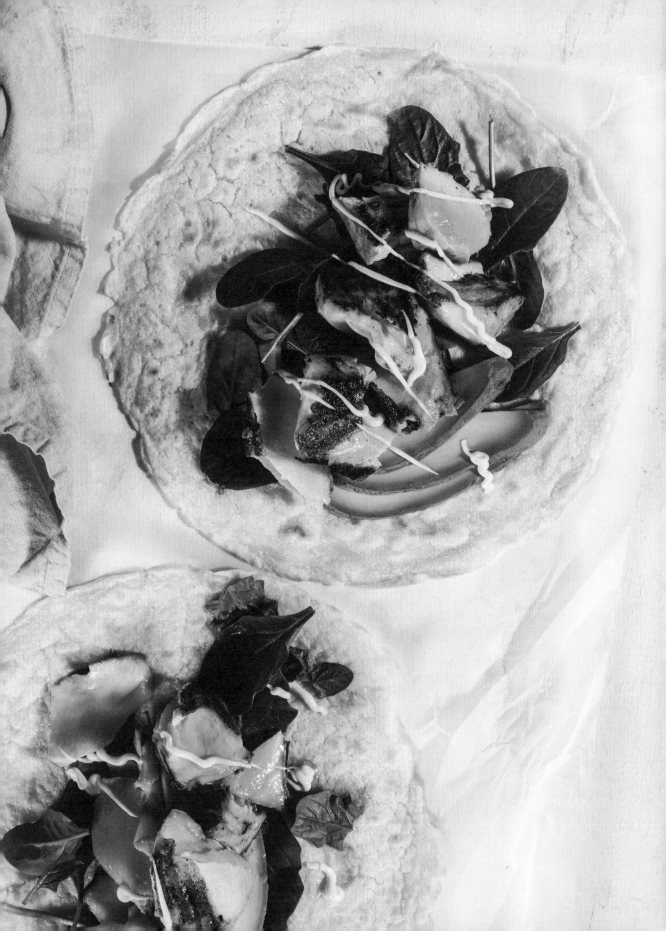

CHILLI PRAWN ZASTA

This is the perfect hump day meal. For the longest time I thought Wednesday was referred to as 'hump day' because people didn't have shit on so they played hide-the-sausage for something to do, i.e. they humped. Nope, Shannon, incorrect, it's nothing to do with fucking, it's because Wednesday is the depressing midpoint of the work week – the climbing of a proverbial hill. Hump day generally correlates with a slump in mood, a need to punch faces and a tolerance for only zero-fucks-given cooking. So here is the ultimate zero-fucks dinner. It is so creamy and tasty, and can be whipped up in less time than it takes to pull a dick.

DO IT

1 Get a frypan or wok heating up over medium-high heat and pop the oil in.

2 Throw in the garlic and give it a little sizzle, then bang the prawns in and give them a good flick around so they're coated in garlic.

3 Now get the chilli in and stir. Don't breathe in the chilli fumes or your nose will get all tingly and weird. Let that all cook for a couple of minutes.

4 When the prawns have just turned opaque (likely just a few minutes), add in the parsley and coconut cream.

5 While this is all bubbling away, get another frypan heating up (on high) to make your zasta. Get the oil in there and when it is hot, throw in the zucchini strips. Sauté for just a minute. Don't let it get all flaccid and disappointing. Add a sprinkle of salt.

6 Let's get back to the prawns. Add in the lemon juice and then have a cheeky sample taste. Does it need more lemon juice? Or perhaps some salt and pepper? If so, whack it in.

7 Serve the prawns on top of the zasta (or normal-person pasta if you so desire) and brace yourself for some tasty business.

Serves 2

FOR THE PRAWNY SAUCE

Wee bit of oil to fry this shit in (I use butter or coconut oil)

2 or 3 cloves garlic, minced

300 g raw prawns (get shelled ones, don't make your life difficult)

3 birdseye chillis, finely chopped, I'm talking FINE AS FUCK

Handful of chopped fresh parsley

1 cup (250 ml) coconut cream

Juice of ½ a lemon (or possibly a full lemon if you're a zesty motherfucker)

Salt and pepper to taste

FOR THE ZASTA*
(FLOG-SPEAK FOR ZUCCHINI PASTA)

3 zucchinis. These mofos need to be cut into pasta-like strips. I just use a julienne peeler to make fettucini like strips or you can use a fancy-fuck spiraliser

1 tablespoon oil or butter

A bee's dick of salt

* If you are not up for the zucchini pasta, I don't give a shit, and feel free to use normal-person pasta. I'm just trying to think of your goddamn bowels and up your veggie intake, you ungrateful fuck.

SHANNON'S MUM'S SPAGHETTI MARINARA

Mum's Marinara is famous among her friends and family and I bloody love it. Whenever I visit home I demand she cooks it. When Mum gave me this recipe, I thought the bugger had written it with a pen of lies. I thought she was trying to clutch onto her flavoursome secret, so when she's old and decrepit I won't put her in a nursing home where she can't access a kitchen to make it for me. A kind of Nanna insurance policy. But she wasn't fucking with me, it's just that she cooks this by feel – she's been cooking it for a quarter of a century. I followed her loose instructions, cooking it time and time again, tinkering with the ingredients until I finally got it mastered. 'That's it!' shouted Mr Shannon, one evening. 'That's Nanna's Marinara!' This meal is a treat. It has fuck-all vegetables, but at least you're getting some bloody iodine and zinc with all that seafood so who the fuck cares? Mum's Marinara makes me happy and I wouldn't dream of disrespecting it by nestling it on a sad bed of zucchini noodles, it deserves to ride dirty – atop proper pasta. But if you want to ruin your own day and make this healthier, then substitute the pasta for sautéed spiralised zucchini, just know that you are a knob and you made my mum cry.

DO IT

1 Righto kids, game on. Heat up a frypan over a medium-high heat, add your oil, then gently sauté the onion until it's transparent (a few minutes).

2 Add in the garlic and cook for a minute. Now whack in the tomatoes, tomato paste, wine, honey, salt, pepper and basil. Mix her up like you're Sir Mixalot.

3 Bring this dreamy as fuck sauce to the boil. Then give it a taste. Does she need more basil? If so add more.

4 Add the marinara mix and prawns and simmer until the seafood is cooked. This will take about 5 minutes but look for the prawns and fish becoming opaque.

5 Stir in the chopped shallots. It's a minutiae of vegetables but it's better than fucking nothing.

6 Add a smidgen at a time of the cornflour thickening mix – you might not need it all, it depends how runny you want it. Simmer for a minute or so, then stir in the cream, then the parsley.

7 Pardon yourself to the bathroom and apply bandaids to your nipples so they do not chafe when you taste this delicious dish.

8 Serve atop some cooked spaghetti that you have bathed in butter and dried basil – because you are a fucking winner.

Serves 6 (or 1 Shannon)

1 tablespoon olive oil (or butter)

1 onion, peeled and finely chopped

3 cloves garlic, finely chopped or minced

2 x 400 g tins chopped tomatoes

3 tablespoons tomato paste

½ cup (125 ml) dry white wine

2 teaspoons honey
(Mum uses old people's sugar aka raw sugar)

Salt and pepper to taste

1 tablespoon dried basil

500 g marinara mix

350 g raw green prawns

6 shallots/spring onions, finely chopped

1 tablespoon cornflour
(mixed with 2 tablespoons water – we'll use this as a thickener)

½ to ¾ cup (125–180 ml) cream
(depends how creamy you like it)

2 tablespoons fresh parsley, chopped

TO SERVE

Cooked spaghetti, sprinkled with basil and a little butter

SWEET & SPICY SALMON BOWLS

I'm currently a stay-at-home mum. Can you picture me? A domestic goddess, with freshly washed hair, prancing around the house in a negligee while preparing special meals for my loves. Haha. NO. Most of the time I'm wearing tracksuit pants and yesterday's bun, fighting the urge to shout, 'For Christ's sake! You people ate yesterday! Why must you fuckfaces continue to demand food from me with such intense regularity?!' Our two little boys, Jack and Herbie, are four and one. So I'm lucky if I even get to shit in peace. They keep us busier than a one-armed rodeo clown with itchy ball-crumbs. This busyness combined with my tendency to give zero fucks means there are many occasions where night falls, and Mr Shannon and I have been ridden hard and put away wet, and we have a 'What the fuck are we going to eat for dinner tonight?' moment. Sweet & Spicy Salmon Bowls has become our go-to meal. It is bloody easy and is mad nipple boner inspo.

DO IT

1 Make the Sweet & Spicy Saucey Bit by mixing all that shit together. The honey can be a little resistant but don't let that sticky fucker get the better of you.

2 Now plonk it over the salmon fillets (you can let them have a marination session if you want to but it's not fucking necessary).

3 When it's dinner time, heat up a frypan over a medium heat and add the peanut oil. Place the salmon in (skin down if you have fillets with skin on). Cook for 3–4 minutes, then pour over the remaining sauce and let it have a little sizzle. Flip those motherfuckers and cook the other side for about 3–4 minutes.

4 Remove the salmon from the pan and cook your beans for a couple of minutes (or until cooked to your liking), then whack in the pak choy, cooking it until it wilts.

5 Plonk the cooked rice in the bottom of your bowls, then drop on those saucy greens and nestle the salmon on top. Any leftover sauce can be poured over the top. Easy as fuck.

Serves 2

THE SWEET & SPICY SAUCEY BIT

¼ cup (90 g) honey

1 tablespoon tahini

1 teaspoon Sriracha sauce

2 teaspoons tamari

OTHER STUFF

2 salmon fillets (can be skin on or off, whatever pleases you)

Peanut oil for cooking (or whatever oil you fancy)

Couple of handfuls of green beans (or whatever veggies you fancy. We actually use frozen mixed veggies when we are feeling especially knackered)

A fuckload of pak choy (I use 2 bunches per person)

A bee's dick of sesame oil

TO SERVE

1 or 2 cups cooked brown rice (depends how greedy you guys are)

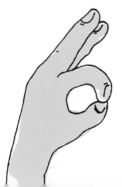

HONEY PRAWNS (SUGARY AS FUCK)

I was lucky enough to have a naughty old lady in my life for many years. We met when I was 16 and she soon became my Bad Granny. One day, I took her shopping for a new bra. 'Excuse me, dear,' she said to the young woman behind the counter, 'can you point me in the direction of the crotchless knickers?' The shopkeeper's mouth fell agape and she stared in disbelief at my innocent-looking granny. 'Oh, it's nothing rude! I just wear them to keep the flies out of my eyes.' I'm pretty sure the shopkeeper shit her pants in horror at this stage. Then my Bad Granny started laughing and assured the poor young lass she was yanking her chain. I think the poor girl had turned her face heavenward and prayed to God that we would just fuck off as we giggled and trotted away to look at old lady bras. She was great fun. She loved giving and receiving cheek, and she loved a strong coffee, a whiskey and prawns. This Honey Prawns recipe is a bit naughty, just like she was, the dear old shit.

DO IT

1 Make the honey sauce first. Melt the butter in a saucepan over low-medium heat, then add in the ginger and garlic. Give it a stir for a minute, until it's smelling nice and potent, then add in the honey. Stir and leave it to lightly simmer while you work on the prawns.

2 Heat the oil in a wok over high heat, then whack your onion in. Flick it around for minute or so, until it turns transparent and slightly golden.

3 Add the veggies and cook for a couple of minutes. Add the prawns into the wok, tossing them regularly. Let them cook until they turn opaque (likely around 2–3 minutes), then pour the honey sauce in. Swill it around so everything gets coated in that sticky sweet shit.

4 Serve atop rice. Don't wear crotchless knickers or you might slip off your seat – this is some tasty business.

Serves 4

THE STIR-FRY BIT

1 tablespoon peanut oil

1 onion, sliced

1 carrot, sliced julienne

1 head broccoli, cut into little florets

20 snow peas, trimmed and diagonally halved

1 red capsicum, thinly sliced

600 g raw green prawns, shelled
(and poo-chutes removed hopefully)

THE HONEY SAUCE BIT

¼ cup (60 g) butter
(YES. That is a fucktonne of butter)

1 teaspoon ginger, minced

2 cloves garlic, minced

½ cup (180 g) honey (sugary as fuck)

TO SERVE

Cooked brown rice

VEGGIE CURRY WITH EGG

When I first moved out of home I was poor as fuck. I was studying at uni and trying to work enough for rent, food, bills and to keep myself flush with $2 shots from Jimmy Rowes. I was so povo I stapled tiny pieces of material together to make curtains. They did not keep the light out or my dignity in. Times were tough. My much-loved friend and I used to have BBQs regularly – not steaks or chops, just the cheapest, dirtiest sausages imaginable. I use the term 'BBQs' loosely. What I mean is we put our electric frypan on an extension cord and took it outside onto the patio. Classy as fuck. Happy as can be. The rest of my diet consisted of chocolate, toast and curries. I was a total curry bandit in those penniless years because they are cheap as fuck. I'm sure they singlehandedly saved me from malnutrition. This ridiculously easy vegetable curry is a mishmash of cuisines and is bloody good, it's one of Mr Shannon's faves.

DO IT

1 Boil your potatoes for about 15 minutes to soften them slightly, they need a head start over the other ingredients, stubborn little fucks. Then drain them into a colander.

2 Brown the onion in a large pot or pan with the oil for a few minutes (until it looks a bit golden).

3 Whack in that shitload of curry paste. DON'T FORGET TO STAND THE FUCK BACK, it's gonna spit like an enraged llama. Give it a minute or two to sizzle away, until it's smelling super aromatic.

4 Now chuck in all your grouse vegetables and stir it around.

5 Add in the coconut milk and stir. Pop the lid on and have that simmer for about 30 minutes, or until the vegetables are soft.

6 When it's ready, serve it atop brown rice, with a smidgen of fresh coriander, and whack a fried egg on top because why the fuck not?

Serves 4

2 potatoes, chopped into little bites

1 onion, chopped

1 tablespoon peanut oil
(or whatever oil you fancy)

Jar (210 g-ish) of Panang curry paste*

½ medium pumpkin, peeled and chopped into little bites

1 medium eggplant, chopped into little bites

1 medium sweet potato, peeled and chopped into little bites

2 cups (500 ml) coconut milk

TO SERVE

Cooked brown rice

4 fried eggs

Fresh coriander, chopped, if you fancy

* not vegetarian as it contains shrimp paste

SMOKEY CAULIFLOWER SOUP WITH MAPLE BACON

I have explored farts quite a bit in my life. As a child, my best friend and I would back up onto varying surfaces to investigate the range of pitches that could be produced. Our research led us to recommend tiles and linoleum as ideal pop-off enhancers. As I grew into young adulthood, another friend and I discovered that you can fart into a plastic bag, quickly seal it, and then woof it under a door into the room of an unsuspecting victim. This is known as fart-bagging. It was with this same friend that our systematic inquiries extended to examine other properties of farts. Are they flammable? Let me tell you, unequivocally, they indeed are. It's one of my favourite memories. My dear (and very attractive) friend laying on her back, knees drawn to her chest, with a lighter at the ready. It was with wide eyes that I witnessed the fire-fart. A miracle of nature. We are now both parents and have become aware the pants she was wearing at the time were not flame retardant, not even a little bit. They were silky Adidas pants and she's lucky to still have a functioning anus. If you want to explore fire-farts yourself, then I recommend eating this soup beforehand, and wearing sensible pants for fuck's sake.

DO IT

1 Preheat your oven to 180°C (fan-forced).

2 Toss the cauliflower in the oil, garlic, garam masala, cinnamon, smoked paprika and cumin.

3 Now get your onion, and toss it in the balsamic vinegar and maple syrup.

4 Throw all of those veggies in a big roasting dish and bake them for about 30–40 minutes, until they're golden brown and a few edges have a slight cheeky char.

5 While they're roasting, make the Cheeky Sprinkler. Just toss the bacon in the maple syrup, and fry over high heat for about 5–10 minutes (until it looks crunchy and lovely). This spits like fuck, so please beware.

6 To make the soup, place your roasted veggies, stock and coconut milk in a blender and whizz the absolute fuck out of it. You want it smooth and creamy.

7 Serve it up with the Cheeky Sprinkler on top.

8 Get your lighter out.

Makes about 4 bowls

THE SOUP BIT

1 head cauliflower, roughly cut into florets

2 tablespoons melted duck fat, ghee or coconut oil

2 cloves garlic, minced

1 teaspoon garam masala

1 teaspoon cinnamon

1 teaspoon smoked paprika

½ teaspoon cumin

2 onions, chopped

1 tablespoon balsamic vinegar

1 tablespoon maple syrup

2 cups (500 ml) chicken stock

1 cup (250 ml) coconut milk

THE CHEEKY SPRINKLER BIT

250 g cubed bacon*

1 tablespoon maple syrup

Smidgen of oil (I use peanut but use whatever you like)

* Clearly this is not a vegetarian dish, sadly bacon counts.

POTATO & ROSEMARY PIZZA

I would consider myself an authority on nipple erections. I believe I have been at maximum boner levels. I have seen just how far that duo of flesh can be pushed. Mine reached their glass-cutting pinnacle in Antarctica. Mr Shannon and I used to be travel bandits and we once scored a cheap, last-minute voyage to the Antarctic Circle. It was aboard an old research boat refashioned into a humble cruiser. The beds were basically tiny rocks and you had to shower over the toilet, but there was a well-stocked bar so zero fucks were given. Each day we would hop in zodiac boats, weave around the icebergs and head to shore to explore that icy fucker by foot. It was otherworldly and spectacular. At the end of the trip, we were offered the opportunity to jump off the side of the ship into the zero-degree water. Appropriate dress would have been a thick-as-fuck wetsuit, or the skin of a local leopard seal, but instead I was ill-equipped with a bikini. As I plunged deep into the water, my bikini top malfunctioned and revealed to all 50 spectators the fiercest and sprightliest set of nipple fats I will ever have in my life. They were off the charts. I'm sure the captain considered tying me to the front of the ship so my nipples could function as ice-breakers. They were really something but the nipple erections you'll get after tasting this simple Potato & Rosemary Pizza are a worthy rival – it's a tasty one.

DO IT

1 Preheat your oven to 190°C (fan-forced).

2 Let's make the base. Drain the quinoa well through a strainer, then whack it in the food processor with the egg, oil and salt. Whizz the shit out of it. You want it to end up looking like smooth sludge.

3 Line a pizza tray with baking paper, and spoon the quinoa batter on, spreading it out to about 30 cm diameter – you want that bastard nice and thin. Pop it in the oven for 15 minutes.

4 Mix up the olive oil, rosemary, garlic, salt and pepper in a large mixing bowl. This is 'the baste'. Whack the thinly-sliced potato in the baste, so it all gets greasy and flavoursome as fuck, then place the potato slices on a baking tray and bake for about 10–15 mins, until they look a little golden.

5 Paint your pizza base with leftover baste-juice and sprinkle on half the cheese. Next layer is the cooked potato, followed by the rest of the cheese on top.

6 Bang that fucker in the oven for another 10 minutes or so, until the cheese is all melted and it looks like pizza perfection.

Makes 1 pizza

⅓ cup (80 ml) olive oil

2 tablespoon fresh rosemary, finely chopped

3 cloves garlic, minced

salt and pepper

2 medium potatoes, thinly sliced
(like, 2 mm thick, thin as fuck)

½ cup (60 g) mozzarella, grated

½ cup (60 g) tasty cheese, grated

THE HEALTHY-AS-FUCK BASE*

1 cup (190 g) quinoa, soaked the fuck out of in water for 8+ hours

1 egg

1 tablespoon olive oil

½ teaspoon salt

* This is some pretty healthy shit, so if you don't want to make this fucker you can use a tastier regular-person thin pre-made pizza base, I don't give a shit. I'm just trying to get some bloody protein and wholegrains into your arse-pipes.

SPICY BEANS WITH CREAMY ROSEMARY GOODNESS

It was a night shift. I was alone in the ED nurses' station at 3 am. Or so I thought. I did a cheeky little pop off, just a sweet little squeaky one with a crisp exit. 'Excellent work, Shannon,' I thought. Next second I hear the shuffling of papers behind me. My neck hairs bristled and I turned around slowly and saw that Dr Handsome was right there. For fuck's sake. So I did what any normal person would do. I tried to get my shoes to catch on the floor in such a way as to replicate a little squeak sound in the hope that Dr Handsome would think the original noise was shoe-related. I gave it my all. To this day I have no idea if my plan was successful. It keeps me up at night. These days I am free to eat as many beans as I like because I am constantly surrounded by my two little boys who I can always blame for any gaseous indiscretions. #blessed

DO IT

1 Heat a large pan over medium heat. Add oil, then the garlic and onion. Give that a couple of minutes until the onion turns slightly golden. Then add the balsamic vinegar and maple syrup. Give that a couple of minutes, stirring a fair bit.

2 Now whack in all the other Beany Bit ingredients, and stir to combine. Pop the lid on the pan, and let that simmer for about 25–30 minutes, or until vegetables are cooked.

3 To make the Creamy Goodness, just whack all the ingredients into a food processor and whizz the fuck out of it until it's smooth. You will have to scrape the sides down every now and then. Sorry 'bout dat.

4 Serve up your Beany Bit with the Creamy Goodness, either on brown rice with shredded greens, or be a dirty fucker and have it with corn/bean chips. No judgement here – I farted in front of a sexy doctor man for fuck's sake, I'm not going to issue any decrees.

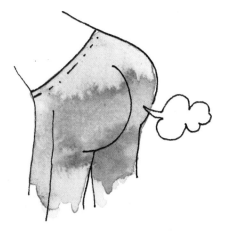

Serves 4

THE BEANY BIT

1 tablespoon oil

2 cloves garlic, finely chopped

1 onion, finely chopped

2 tablespoons balsamic vinegar

1 tablespoon maple syrup

1 x 400 g tin lentils, drained and rinsed

300 g salsa

½ an eggplant, finely chopped

1 carrot, finely chopped

1 zucchini, finely chopped

1 red capsicum, finely chopped

1 teaspoon Sriracha sauce
(add more if you're a spice bandit)

1 teaspoon smoked paprika

THE CREAMY GOODNESS

1 cup (150 g) cashews, soaked for 6+ hours

1 avocado

Juice of 1 lemon

2 teaspoons maple syrup

½ cup (125 ml) milk (cow, coconut, whatever)

Leaves off 2 dick-length sprigs of rosemary
(as always, reference is to erect peens)

A bee's dick of salt

TO SERVE

Brown rice and shredded greens OR you can be a total flavour legend and have corn/bean chips. Don't fuck it up though – choose a decently-made chip that doesn't contain a fucktonne of added salt and shit

RED VEGAN STEW WITH MASH

Your eyes are a window to your soul, and your buttonhole is a window to your health – you can tell a fair bit from your shit. Is it sticking to your brown sunflower as though it came out sideways? Is it so adhesive that the Liquid Nails company is sniffing around trying to patent its formulation? Did it mistake your anus for a sheep's and come out in little rock-nuggets of doom? Would it be easier to birth a human baby than this food baby? If so, chances are you need to eat more fucking vegetables. While I understand there has never been a more unappealing combination than 'vegan' and 'stew', don't roll your eyes like a fuckstick and turn the page in a rage. Give this recipe a bloody chance – Red Vegan Stew is inexpensive, healthy as fuck and could possibly give you the best shit of your life. I'm talking big enough to choke a small donkey but with a low stink factor and only one wipe required, vis-a-vis, a dream shit. If the promise of launching an amazing arse rocket isn't enough to entice you, then know that this is the easiest bloody thing in the world to cook.

DO IT

1 Heat up a large frypan on a medium-high heat, and plop in some oil when it's hot.

2 Fry the garlic, eggplant and capsicum for about 5 minutes, until it's got a golden tinge and a wee bit of charring on the eggplant.

3 Now whack in the balsamic vinegar and honey, and give it a stir for about 2 minutes and watch it get a little sticky.

4 Then whack in the beans, tomatoes, tomato paste and salt. Bring to a simmer. Turn the heat down and keep it gently simmering for about 30 minutes with the lid on.

5 Stir through the parsley.

6 Serve it up with some fluffy mashed potato.

Serves about 6

Oil of your choice

3 cloves garlic, finely chopped

2 eggplants, cut into bite-sized chunks

2 capsicums, cut into bite-sized chunks

3 tablespoons balsamic vinegar

2 tablespoons honey (or maple syrup if you're serving a devout vegan)

1 x 400 g tin cannellini beans, drained and rinsed

2 x 400 g tins diced tomatoes

2 tablespoons tomato paste

A bee's dick of salt

½ cup fresh parsley, chopped

TO SERVE

Mashed potato (if you're whipping this up for a vegan, use almond milk and coconut oil instead of butter and milk. And don't forget the salt and pepper, for fuck's sake)

CHICKEN
SHIT

CHICKEN WITH TASTY TURMERIC CAULIFLOWER PUREE

Rio de Janeiro is my favourite city. Fun and a bit wild, but friendly. When I was there, I decided to go hang gliding. Jumping off a cliff harnessed into a glider with a strange man – what could go wrong? I wasn't feeling nervous about it at all until I saw the car that was driving the glider, the instructor, assistant and me to the mountain top. It looked like a decrepit 1978 piece of shit. Looks can be deceiving but in this case they were not. They were spot-fucking-on. The car struggled and strained, stalling and rolling back down, time and again. I can tell you, this did absolutely nothing to inspire my confidence in their entire operation. I felt certain I was going to plunge to my untimely death. But they won me back by using ingenuity – they decided to try reversing up. It bloody worked. We reversed up the mountain and arrived to a spectacular view of that beautiful city. A quick strap into the glider, a wee sprint off the edge of the cliff and we were away. The glide down was flawless and unforgettable. So, sometimes the journey is fucked but the result is worth it. This recipe is the same: a bit of a ball-ache to make but a wise investment of your time. Please don't let the idea of turmeric cauliflower put you off, this recipe is just so damn tasty.

DO IT

1 Mix up the marinade and whack the chicken in there. Best left for a few hours but if you have zero time and/or fucks it's fine with just a short soak.

2 Get your cauliflower steaming. Steam for about 20–25 minutes or until a fork can poke into it as easy as shit. Then transfer the cauliflower to a food processor or blender and add in the yoghurt, lemon juice, honey, turmeric, cumin, butter, salt and pepper. Whizz it until it looks mashy and creamy.

3 While your cauliflower is steaming, heat up a frypan to medium-high heat and pour a smidgen of oil in there. Get the chicken thighs in and cook for about 10 minutes (or until cooked through), turning every now and then. Whack your beans in to cook for the last few minutes.

4 Slice the chicken and serve it on a bed of that crazy puree with the beans nestled alongside. Squirt a cheeky bit of Sriracha on there. Healthy as fuck! It looks as ugly as a hat full of arseholes but, by Jesus, is it damn tasty.

Serves 3 or 4

600 g chicken thighs

4 big handfuls of green beans

Olive oil

THE MARINADEY BIT

1 tablespoon olive oil

1 teaspoon dried oregano

1 teaspoon ground coriander

Juice of ½ a lemon

2 cloves garlic, minced

THE CAULIFLOWER BIT

1 head cauliflower, cut into florets. You can cut up some of the stem too

½ cup (140 g) plain yoghurt

¼ cup (60 ml) lemon juice

1 teaspoon honey

1 teaspoon ground turmeric

1 teaspoon cumin

2 teaspoons butter

Salt and pepper to taste (I suggest a fair whack of salt)

TO SERVE

Sriracha sauce (NOT optional. It is essential. Fucking essential)

FEELING LIKE SHIT CHICKEN SOUP

Sometimes we get sick and we just bloody want a bloody cuddle from our mums and some goddamn chicken soup. When my second child was born he had to be sliced out. When the surgeon lifted him skyward like Simba from *The Lion King*, I expected the 'Circe of Life' song to start blasting – but all I heard was my fanny sigh with relief because it didn't have to squeeze that giant human meatball out. My abdomen was less delighted with the situation and I was feeling about as fresh as a pair of balls three days into a music festival. As soon as Mum came in and asked what she could do for me I put my hand up for chicken soup. This soup is a saviour cos it's pretty light on the tummy. It's friggin' tasty too – this son of a bitch's herb and spice usage would impress Colonel Sanders. It takes a bit of time to make but it's worth it. It's kind of like pho meets Grandma-style chicken soup.

DO IT

1 Heat a soup pot over a high heat, add in some butter and then fry up the onion, lemongrass, chilli, garlic and ginger for a few minutes. Now plonk the star anise, cloves, cinnamon stick and coriander seeds in the pot and give it a quick stir. The poor chook goes in next. Cover it with the water and pour in the apple cider vinegar.

2 Bring this to a boil, then turn the heat down so it's just simmering, and leave it for 1.5 hours.

3 Pull the chicken out. It might fall apart like Carrie Bradshaw did EVERY SINGLE TIME Big left her so don't let a chunk of it slip out of your mitts and fall on the floor. Place it on a plate and pull the meat off the bones and put aside, then return the bones to the pot to boil away for another 2 hours.

4 When those bones have had enough time to flavour and nourish the stock, pour the stock into a large bowl through a sieve, to catch all the chunky bits, then return the clear stock back to the pot and add in the fish sauce and lemon juice.

5 To serve, place cooked rice noodles and chicken (and zucchini if you're greening it up) in the base of each bowl and pour the stock over the top. Sprinkle with fresh coriander and whack a lemon wedge on top.

Serves 4–6

1 tablespoon butter (or fat of your choice)

2 onions, roughly chopped

1 stalk lemongrass, roughly chop the white part and piff the rest

3 long red chillis, roughly chopped

6 cloves garlic, roughly chopped

6 square cm ginger, roughly chopped

6 star anise

6 cloves

1 cinnamon stick

2 tablespoons coriander seeds

1 medium whole raw chicken

12 cups (3 litres) water

1 tablespoon apple cider vinegar

2 tablespoons fish sauce

Juice of 1 lemon (or lime)

TO SERVE

Rice noodles, soaked in boiling water until soft

Fresh coriander

Lemon (or lime) wedges

Optional – zucchini, peeled into noodles

CHICKEN SATAY

'You can, ah . . . you can give it a little rub if you like,' said the dear, weak old man mid bed-bath. He was my patient, I was his nurse. He was talking about his dick, which I was about to wash. I don't know why old men delude themselves into thinking young nurses have a sexual fever that can only be cured by handling ageing knobs but they sometimes give it a fucking go. Good on them, I suppose. 'Oh mate, they barely pay me enough to wash the damn thing, let alone tug it.' He nodded graciously in understanding and we went about our usual business and chatted about the weather and politics. Bless him, but dry old sausage is just not that enticing, and neither is a dry old satay, so this recipe is a moist and tasty one. But flavour and moisture alone won't get us to old age. So I eat healthy shit like this Chicken Satay because one day I want to be an old tart soliciting crotch touches of my own. Enjoy.

DO IT

1 Heat a saucepan over medium heat, and plonk in the peanut oil, then add in the chilli and garlic and fry up for a minute or so. Pour in the honey and peanut butter and stir it round and get it all melty. Then add in the tamari, fish sauce and coconut milk and whisk it until it's combined.

2 Heat a wok over high heat, and place the peanut oil in. Get the onion in there and fry until transparent and slightly golden. Then chuck the chicken, zucchini and broccoli in and fry for about 5 minutes (or until chicken and vegetables are cooked to your liking) then throw the satay sauce and pak choy in and cook until it wilts (about a minute).

3 Serve atop cooked brown rice and say a little prayer for all the poor nurses out there having to dodge old dick at work.

Serves about 4

THE SATAY SAUCE

1 tablespoon peanut oil

3 birdseye chillis, finely chopped
(less if you don't like spicy shit)

2 cloves garlic, finely chopped

2 tablespoons honey

5 tablespoons peanut butter

1 tablespoon tamari

1 tablespoon fish sauce

1 cup (250 ml) coconut milk

OTHER BITS

1 tablespoon peanut oil

1 onion, diced

500 g chicken thighs, chopped into
bite-sized chunks

2 zucchini, cut into half moons

1 head broccoli, cut into florets

1 bunch pak choy, roughly chopped

TO SERVE

Cooked brown rice

CHICKEN STIR-FRY

Years back, Mr Shannon and I went to Thailand for a getaway. One day, hungover as fuck, we thought we would treat ourselves with a massage. We chose one that looked respectable. There were Nannas downstairs getting pedicures for fuck's sake. I realised something was askew when showering was required before the massage and the masseuse CAME IN while I was showering. There was no averting of eyes or a 'Oh! Pardon me!', she just waltzed around the room while I tried to wash my gear. After showering, I lay face down on the table, feebly attempting to cover myself with a tiny, decrepit towel. The masseuse whipped the towel off and promptly gave my bottom a pert smack, declaring my little panties to be 'Sexy!'*****. At this point I knew I was in trouble. At the turnover point my heart began to race. She massaged my titties. Hmm, not bad, and I didn't want to offend so I kept my mouth (and thighs) shut. Then the drive-bys started. Gentle, possibly unintended grazings of the crotchal region. 'Should I say something? Or is this accidental?' I thought. Then she started making contact with my loinchops in a manner akin to trying to get mud off a tyre. JESUS. 'I'm ok! Thanks! But I'm ok,' I said awkwardly while wildly flailing my arms. But what about Mr Shannon? That's a story for a therapist or someone with beer and Valium. Anyway, it wasn't all rub and tugs in Thailand. We also ate a lot of good food. There was one chicken cashew dish I adored and I have tried to recreate it here. Genital touching optional.

DO IT

1 Get your blender or food processor out and give him a cheeky bit of advice: 'Bring your A-game, you son of a bitch'. Put the Saucy Component ingredients into the food processor and set it to 'Maximum Whizz'. Give it some shit until it looks like a thick sauce.

2 Heat up the oil in a wok over high heat, then get the chicken in there. Toss it around until it's almost cooked, then take it out and put it aside for later.

3 It's onion's turn to get in the wok. Throw it in and give it a bit of a browning. Once it's a bit golden, add in the rest of your veggies. Keep tossing and stirring them around for a minute, then add in the sauce. Await the sizzle and don't burn your damn self.

4 The veggies won't take long to cook, just a matter of 2 or 3 minutes. You don't want them all soggy and flaccid as fuck.

5 Chuck the chicken back in there to warm up for a minute.

6 That's it, you're done! Serve it on brown rice, and sprinkle the cashews and coriander on top.

7 Attempt to conceal your stiffie, unless you're in the company of one who enjoys it, in which case, present it.

* Pre-children I used to wear beautiful little knickers, you know the ones that come on their own little hanger? Now I wear 5 packs from Big W.

Serves 2

THE MEATY BIT

2 teaspoons peanut oil

Few cheeky drops of sesame oil

300 g chicken thigh, sliced nice and thin

1 red capsicum, sliced

¾ brown onion, sliced
(use the rest in the sauce)

1 carrot, cut into little sticks

1 small head broccoli, cut into florets

THE SAUCY COMPONENT

1 red capsicum

¼ brown onion

4 pitted Medjool dates

1 teaspoon grated ginger

1 clove garlic, minced

1 birdseye chilli, chopped fine as fuck

Juice of 1 lime

A bee's dick of salt

TO SERVE

Cooked brown rice

Couple of handfuls of cashews, roasted

Handful of fresh coriander, chopped

BAKED KINDA-LIKE BUTTER CHICKEN

'Shannon! Where are the fucking vegetables?' They have fucked right off because it's our tastebuds' turn for some fun. The veggies have fucked waaaaay off. Then we said, 'Oi, back further, go on, you heard me, fuck off! You'll just ruin this dish.' Then tomato and onion gave us a little wink and we said, 'Ohh, righto boys, you can get in but the rest of you keep fucking off. Nope. Not far enough. Fuck off some more.' And so they fucked right off and we were happy. I can understand that you may want to extend this message of fuck-offery to me when you look at the ingredients list. Yes, it's true that you may have to spend half of your life savings to purchase all of these spices, but once you have them in your pantry you will never look back. Except to check behind you for all the uninvited stiffies that will be coming at you once people get wind of your mad cooking skills. This is a very, very tasty dish.

DO IT

1 Preheat your oven to 180°C (fan-forced).

2 Make your curry paste by adding all that shit into a food processor and whizzing the fuck out of it. If you don't have a food processor then cry yourself a river and chop the fuck out of all the solid shit, then stir it all together like a peasant.

3 Get yourself a big-arse pot (with a lid) that you can bang both on the stovetop and in the oven, what I would like to call 'a double-banger'. I just use a soup pot. Heat the double-banger over a high heat, then add in your butter. When that's all melted and hissy, put in your curry paste. STAND THE FUCK BACK. That shit is going to sizzle. Stir that around for a minute or two, and once it's smelling so ridiculously aromatic that you have procured two nipple erections, add in the onion. Let that brown for a minute before adding the chicken. Give that about 5 minutes to brown up a smidgen.

4 Ok, now take that off the heat and throw in the rest: the tomatoes, honey, cinnamon, star anise and cloves. Give it a wee little stir, put the lid on, then put the double-banger in the oven and catch it later. About 30 minutes later.

5 Stir coconut cream through, then serve it up with rice and fresh coriander and await the barrage of erectile tissue that will soon point in your direction when your guests taste this awesome spicy chicken. Bat away erectile tissue belonging to unattractive persons with silverware.

Serves about 6

THE CURRY PASTE BIT

6 square cm ginger

4 cloves garlic

3 long red chillis

⅓ cup (80 ml) apple cider vinegar

½ cup (140 g) tomato paste

1 teaspoon cumin powder

1 tablespoon smoked paprika

2 teaspoons garam masala

THE REST

Several tablespoons butter or ghee

2 brown onions, chopped

1 kg chicken thighs, chopped into bite-sized chunks

1 x 400 g tin chopped tomatoes

¼ cup (90 g) honey

2 cinnamon sticks

2 star anise

2 cloves

1 cup (250 ml) coconut cream

TO SERVE

Cooked brown basmati rice

Coriander to serve, if you're a flash cunt, which I imagine you are

GRAINLESS LAMB BURGERS

FUCKS GIVEN  TASTINESS

'Do you want to see how I did it? I have a video,' the patient enquired. I pondered the question, 'Ahh no, I don't think that's necessary.' *It definitely wasn't necessary.* 'Are you sure?' *Yes, dear man, I am quite sure I don't need to see a video of you breaking your penis but thank you for the kind offer.* I'm not sure what feat he was expecting to capture when he decided to film himself playing hide the sausage with his partner but I'm sure it wasn't a snapped piss-weasel. Working in the emergency department of a busy Melbourne hospital was interesting. And stressful at times. In fact, I even started referring to burgers as 'stress burgers' – eating junk food had become a way to cope. Every day had challenges. Not all testing moments involved people's busted-up privates though, sometimes it was just awful stuff like failed CPR or some dirty fuck spitting at you. But burgers to the rescue! I'm quite sure I ate my bodyweight in burgers in those days. I still adore them but now I'm a health conscious knob who makes more nutritious versions, like this tasty lamb burger. No need to save this as a calming treat after observing a broken pizzle, you can have it any ol' time.

DO IT

1 To make The Lamb Bit, mix the mince and relish together. Then divide the mixture in half and make it into two little patties. You have to really smoosh that shit together with your hands to make it stick, otherwise the patties will fall apart when you cook them.

2 Preheat the oven to 180°C (fan-forced).

3 Whack all of the bun ingredients (except the seeds) in a bowl and whisk like a crazy motherfucker until it's smooth and perfect.

4 Line a baking tray with baking paper and divide the mixture into four equal blobs on the baking paper. Sprinkle the sesame seeds on two (two are bottoms, two are tops. I think if I was a bun I would definitely be a top).

5 Whack it straight into the oven and bake for 10–12 minutes (look for the buns turning golden brown all over, more so on the edges). When they're cooked, pop them on a cooling rack.

6 While they're baking, cook the meat. Heat up a frypan over high heat and whack in some oil. Cook them for about 10 minutes, flipping as needed, give or take depending how well done you like your patties. If you opted for cheese, pop it on a couple of minutes before they're cooked so it slightly melts.

7 Assemble your burger with the mayo, relish, avocado, onion, tomato, patties and green shit.

8 Chomp it.

* Look, I'm not going to lie to you, these are some flat-arse little buns. They're not fluffy, but they actually go fucking alright. Even Mr Shannon prefers these grainless fucks to normal buns now.

Serves 2

THE LAMB BIT

250 g lamb mince

2 tablespoons tomato relish

Oil to cook those fuckers

THE BUNS*

4 eggs

¼ cup (30 g) almond meal

¼ cup (35 g) tapioca flour

2 tablespoons coconut flour

2 tablespoons melted coconut oil or butter

1 teaspoon honey

¼ teaspoon baking powder

A bee's dick of salt

Sprinkle of sesame seeds

THE HERBY MAYO

¼ cup (75 g) Kewpie mayo

An epic sprinkle of mixed herbs (just keep dippin' your finger in and sampling until you have nailed the herb levels)

Optional – a bee's dick of lemon juice

OTHER BURGER BITS

Tomato relish

½ an avocado, slightly mashed

Red onion, sliced into rings

Tomato, sliced

Green shit of your choice – some sort of lettuce or baby spinach situation

Optional – tasty cheese

SLOW-COOKED BEEF STROGANOFF

There is a man other than Mr Shannon who holds the key to my heart. His name is French Shane Crawford. I saw him from a distance as he danced on stage at Moulin Rouge. He looked like a young Shane Crawford, besieged by the sparkliest sequins imaginable. He was a vision. He danced like an angel but when we first made eye contact and he offered me a sensual wink, I knew that he was anything but. When patrons were seated, the men were sat facing away from the stage, with their female accompaniment across from them afforded the full view. There were many women's eyes boring into the back of their gent's skulls as the men tried their best to look casual and uninterested while they ogled young bouncing titties – but their eye-stiffies were very poorly veiled. Mr Shannon may have had eye-stiffies too, frankly I didn't give a damn. I had eye-stiffies of my own for French Shane Crawford. What has French Shane Crawford got to do with Beef Stroganoff? Well, nothing. Except that it was in France when I crossed back over to the dark side – I gave up vegetarianism and ate red meat like a fucking king. This isn't chewy swill you'd expect from some shithouse cabaret show though, this dish is delicious as all fuck and is as tender as my heart is for French Shane Crawford.

DO IT

1 Preheat your oven to 90°C (fan-forced) or whack your slow-cooker on low. Grab out a large pot (that has a lid), place it over a medium-high heat and whack in the butter, let it melt, then add in the onion, garlic and steak, and cook for about 5 minutes to let it brown. Give it the occasional stir.

2 Take it off the heat and add in the mushrooms, salt, paprika, tomato paste, Dijon mustard and chicken stock. Stir it all up. Pop the lid on and bang it in the oven for 8 hours (or your slow-cooker).

3 When it's dinner time, stir through the sour cream, then serve it up with the mash or puree (and a wee bit of parsley if you're feeling like jazzing that motherfucker up).

Serves 4–6

2 tablespoons butter (or olive oil if you prefer)

1 onion, diced

5 cloves garlic, minced

600 g oyster blade steak, diced

500 g mushrooms, sliced

½ teaspoon salt

2 teaspoons paprika

2 tablespoons tomato paste

1 tablespoon Dijon mustard

¾ cup (180 ml) chicken stock

¾ cup (180 g) sour cream

TO SERVE

Mashed potato or pureed cauliflower

Smidgen of fresh parsley if you're keen

PULLED PORK FOR PISSPOTS

Once upon a time, as a young Shannon, I was a bit of a dick. It was my 26th birthday and I was travelling in South America. The day started at sunrise, exploring the sensational Bolivian salt flats amid the Andes, and ended at the Extreme Fun Pub in Uyuni. At this fine establishment they offered a delightful 'drinking challenge', which from my sketchy memory entailed an absolute fuckload of shots and beers, some ridiculous flaming blue number and a significant risk of permanent brain injury. Well, if that's not an irresistible way to celebrate a birthday I don't know what is! I partook. What a knob. By the evening's end, I had vomited on my own breasts, my shoes and also into a filthy urinal. I found out about the urinal part because one of my friends showed me a photo of me leaning on it, grinning like a fuckwit. DEAR GOD. Best birthday ever. Ahhhh, Australians . . . We sure do have a drinking problem. So, what better way to celebrate this sick cultural phenomenon than by embracing it in the kitchen?! This slow-cooked number is a piece of piss and bloody tasty.

DO IT

1 Preheat the oven to 200°C (fan-forced).

2 Mix the saucey stuff together.

3 Score the fat of the pork and rub in the salt and smoked paprika.

4 Pour a fair whack of olive oil into a big-arse roasting tray and preheat it for 5 minutes in the oven, then pull it out and place the pork in the tray. Cook for 30 minutes.

5 Pull the tray out and pour over the sauce. Now cover that big fucking tray with foil so it stays moist and lovely. Reduce the oven to 100°C and cook for another 7.5 hours.

6 After that epic slow-roasting session, pull the meat apart and stir it through all the sauce it was roasting in.

7 Assemble your slaw by just mixing all that shit together. Easy as fuck.

8 Serve the pork with brown rice and the slaw or pop it in a roll (or if you have the fucks to give, snuggle it all up in a healthy wrap).

9 Don't have so much Pulled Pork For Pisspots you end up ruining your shoes and dignity. We all like to have fun but the best kind of fun is safe fun.

Serves about 6

2 kg boneless pork shoulder

1 teaspoon salt

1 tablespoon smoked paprika

Olive oil

THE SAUCEY BIT

⅓ cup (80 ml) maple syrup

1 cup (280 g) tomato paste

1 cup (250 ml) spiced rum

1 cup (250 ml) chicken stock

¼ cup (60 ml) balsamic vinegar

1 tablespoon smoked paprika

1 teaspoon ground ginger

THE SLAW BIT

1 Chinese cabbage (wombok), very finely sliced

1 carrot, very finely sliced

1 cup spinach or kale, finely sliced

1 red onion, very finely sliced

4 apples, cored and very finely sliced

Juice of ½ lemon

Kewpie mayonnaise to taste

Sprinkle of ground cumin

TO SERVE

Cooked brown rice, or those delicious wraps from the Miso Salmon Wraps (see page 70) or if you're a really cheeky fuck you can pop it in a brioche roll, but you didn't hear that from me

MELT IN YOUR MOUTH BEEF CURRY

I'm mad on curry. When I was at university, I waitressed in an Indian restaurant. I fucking loved it because I got to eat free curries three or four nights a week. Don't get too excited for me though, I was being paid a pitiful $10 an hour but the chef let me peek over his shoulder when he was cooking and treated me like a little queen (a very underpaid queen). It was a great job, even though chef-man laughed at me when I said I couldn't eat goats because they were my friends. 'And cows? They're not your friends?' Good point. 'Well, yeah, but I tasted them before I realised.' The smells and sights in that kitchen fuelled my curry love. So, here you're going to make your own curry paste. Don't get all, 'Fuck you Shannon! I'm here for the easy shit, I don't have the fucks to give to be making my own curry paste like some sort of kitchen enthusiast!' I hear you. I've been there. But once you gather your collection of herbs and spices and enter the magical world of DIY curries, you'll have the spicy world by the balls, and you'll be loving yourself sick. Unless you don't like spicy food . . . in which case you can go fuck yourself. This Melt In Your Mouth Beef Curry is so tender you can tell that son of a bitch jaw of yours to take the fucking day off.

DO IT

1 Preheat your oven to 170°C (fan-forced).

2 Put the coriander seeds, mustard seeds and cumin seeds into a dry saucepan and give them a little toasting over high heat for a couple of minutes. They'll start to smell lovely and aromatic.

3 Get your food processor out and whizz those toasted seeds until they're powdery. Then add in all of the other curry paste ingredients and give it a whizzing. It'll still look a bit chunky but fuck yeah you just made curry paste, you legendary curry bandit.

4 Grab a large pot with a lid that can go in the oven and transfer the curry paste into it, then plonk in the tomatoes and stock and give her a little stir. Then throw those big-arse pieces of beef in there as well as the eggplant and cinnamon sticks and star anise.

5 Now whack the lid on and throw that cunt straight into the oven. Leave it there for 3 or 4 hours. That's it, mate.

6 When you get it out of the oven, just pull the beef slightly and it'll fall apart. Serve it up with some rice and throw some fresh coriander leaves on top like a culinary boss.

Serves 6

THE CURRY PASTE BIT

2 tablespoons coriander seeds

2 tablespoons mustard seeds

1 tablespoon cumin seeds

2 tablespoons smoked paprika

4 long red chillis

4 cloves garlic

About 6–9 square cm of ginger. That is a lot of fucking ginger but it doesn't end up tasting gingery so be cool

½ cup (140 g) tomato paste

1 tablespoon coconut oil or ghee or butter

⅓ cup (80 ml) apple cider vinegar

1 tablespoon maple syrup

THE REST

2 x 400 g cans diced tomatoes

2 ½ cups (625 ml) chicken stock
(or beef or lamb, whatever you have)

1.2 kg oyster blade beef fillets,
you don't even have to cut that shit

1 eggplant, diced

2 cinnamon sticks

3 star anise

TO SERVE

Fresh coriander leaves

Cooked brown rice

MY BESTIE'S GLAZED HAM

This could be thought of as edible bowel cancer. It's a fucking giant leg of ham covered in sugar and cooked over smoke. But it is so bloody tasty you will proceed regardless. This could be a Christmas staple, or a fancy-arse recipe you pull out for a BBQ just to show your friends who is their culinary overlord. You could serve it up with roasted vegetables, or an ensemble of flashy salads, or just be a fucking champion and put it in a toasted cheese sandwich and call it a fucking day. This glazed ham is so tender, so tasty, so perfect, just like my beautiful friend Mel who cooks it. It's her family recipe and those fuckers can cook. Best you pop on your safety goggles when you serve this up or you may find yourself with a dose of pink-eye from all the chubbies erupting in your direction. You've been warned.

DO IT

1 Get a kettle BBQ going for a delicious smokey flavour (but this can also be cooked in a hot oven).

2 Remove the rind from the giant ham and score the fat in a criss-cross pattern.

3 Mix together the orange juice, mustard, honey and maple syrup to make the glaze.

4 Rub some of that shit all over the ham. There will be heaps left over. Don't throw it out you crazy fucker, keep it for later, you're going to be basting like a bandit.

5 Plonk the ham on a piping hot BBQ (with a tray underneath) and cover.

6 This motherfucker is going to need basting with a brush as often as you remember.

7 Keep basting and cooking for about 2 hours.

8 When it's ready, it should carve up like a dream (pretty much like Prince on the dance floor but with more fat).

9 You might end up with bowel cancer but by fuck you'll have a smile on your face regardless.

Serves . . . umm . . . I don't fucking know. I'm going to say lots.

1 large juicy lookin' orange. Give it a squeeze. Does it feel like a titty? If yes, then it's the one. Juice it

2 heaped tablespoons wholegrain mustard

½ cup (175 g) honey

½ cup (125 ml) maple syrup (so much sugar . . . hence the 3 nipple erections rating)

A big-arse bone-in ham (will likely be about 5 kg). Unless it's Christmas time, you'll probably have to order this from your butcher or supermarket

SLOW-ROASTED GREEK LAMB SHOULDER

The first time I had slow-roasted lamb shoulder was at a restaurant in Melbourne called Cumulus. When it made contact with my tastebuds and I realised just how fucking tender it was, my crotchal region started to get squelchy. As I chewed on, I had to remove my napkin from my lap and place it on my seat, for fear of tarnishing the chair with all of my appreciative secretions. A beach towel would have been a more appropriate receptacle, in all honesty. The napkin was not up for the task but I had to do something. I was either going to cause irreparable harm to the chair or slip straight off the bastard. The meal was that bloody delicious and was the start of my love affair with slow-roasted lamb. I have cooked countless slow-roasts since that moist and enlightening day. A solid three nipple rating for this one. BYO beach towel. And maybe some sticky-tape to seal jizz-holes.

DO IT

1 The day before (if possible), cover the lamb in The Rub Bit. Get into every nook and cranny. Wrap it up and return it to the fridge for a snooze. If you don't have enough time to let it soak, don't stress, it'll still be awesome.

2 Before cooking the lamb, leave it on the bench for a few hours and let it get to room temperature.

3 Preheat your oven to 150°C (fan-forced).

4 Place the lamb in a roasting dish and add in 1 cup of water. Cover the dish with foil and whack it in the oven for 2 hours.

5 Then turn the oven down to 110°C and roast for a further 6 hours but at the 5-hour mark take the foil off and let that fucker bake topless for an hour to crisp up a little.

6 Take the lamb out of the oven and place it on a carving tray, and cover it with foil. Leave it to rest, it won't turn to shit. Turn the oven right the fuck up to 190°C.

7 In another roasting dish, whack in the vegetables and olive oil and toss it all around to coat. Then sprinkle on the lemon rind and rosemary.

8 Roast for about 40 minutes or until golden with slightly charred edges.

9 Add in the olives and feta, and roast for a further 5 minutes.

10 Serve it up. You won't need to carve the lamb, just pull at it with tongs or a fork.

11 Apply towels to your chairs as necessary.

Serves about 6 (or 1 Mr Shannon)

Lamb shoulder, bone in (you want it at least 2 kg, preferably 2.5 kg)

THE RUB BIT

3 tablespoons (60 ml) olive oil

1 tablespoon chopped fresh rosemary

1 tablespoon chopped fresh oregano

4 cloves garlic, finely chopped

Juice of 1 lemon (save the skin for The Non-Meaty Bit)

THE NON-MEATY BIT*

1 Kent pumpkin, peeled and chopped

2 capsicums, sliced

2 onions, peeled and sliced into fat rings

3 zucchini, sliced into rings (about 2cm thick)

1–2 tablespoons olive oil

Zest of 1 lemon

1 tablespoon fresh rosemary, chopped

Few handfuls of pitted kalamata olives

About 200 g hard Greek feta, sliced into little bites

* If you're cooking for fewer people, then just reduce all this non-meaty shit and save the lamb leftovers to make lamb souvlakis. Otherwise leftover veggies can be turned into a soup or thrown into a salad.

HOW I COOK
A GROUSE STEAK

Inside the stable, a mouse was stuck in a pool of dark molasses on the feed-room floor. He'd been there for some time, he was thrashing slowly and weakly, and he had ants crawling all over him. When I saw the poor wee fucker, I bent down to rescue him, then remembered I'm deathly allergic to ant bites, so I did what any kid would do: 'DAAAAAAAAAAAD! DAD!' I bolted out of the stable shouting for my dad. Dad followed me back in, lifted the mouse by his tail and put him in a bucket. He stuck to the bottom of the bucket like shit to a blanket. Ants came with him like an unstoppable rebel force of tiny chomping arseholes. 'We'll give him a little wash,' Dad said, betraying his farming roots. We rinsed the mouse until the ants and molasses were gone. The mouse was in shock, and likely a little cold. Dad cupped him in his strong, calloused hands, giving heat. The mouse sat quietly, shivering. I marvelled at how such a tiny creature could feel safe in a tough bloke's giant paws. That feeling was soon shattered when the mouse suddenly let rip with an almighty bite, drawing blood from two perfect little teethmarks in Dad's hand. 'Dry yourself then, you ungrateful little bastard!' It's a memory that brings me great joy. Probably less so to Dad. Other iconic memories of Dad place him in front of the BBQ, tongs in hand. Many people think their dad cooks the best BBQ but they're all fucking incorrect because MY dad does. I've watched his style over the years and pinched some of his techniques. This is how I cook a steak.*****

DO IT

1 Get your steak out of the fridge an hour or two before cooking time, you want it to be at room temperature when you cook it.

2 Season your steak well with salt.

3 Have the frypan or BBQ fucking hot. If you're using a frypan you'll need to let it heat up for at least 5 minutes, you want it to be slightly smoking.

4 Put the oil or fat in and let that get hot as fuck before you whack the steak in.

5 Flip your steak every 30 seconds or so. Just keep flipping that thing like a goddamn pancake. If you want it medium-rare then a steak of 1 inch thickness will only need 4 or 5 minutes. If you want it cooked more than that then you can just fuck off and have a rissole, you don't deserve a good piece of steak.

6 Remove from the pan or grill and let it rest for 5 minutes after cooking, preferably on a rack.

* There are different ways to cook a steak and I'm not saying this is the one and only correct method but it works a fucking treat for me. I'll happily swim laps in hater's tears because this technique gets me a ripper steak every goddamn time.

Serves 1

Steak of your choice
(I love scotch fillet and eye fillet)

Salt

Oil or fat of your choice

SNACKY & SWEET SHIT

SWEET POTATO CHIPS WITH LIMEY MAYO

Normally a chip imitator deserves a swift smack to the chops – they're generally useless, soggy fucks. They leave me with more bitter disappointment than that time I tried to mount Mr Shannon after he'd consumed the best part of a slab of beer. I've learned my lesson on both fronts – don't expect a decent stiffie from a 20-beer dick, and don't expect to get a decent chip (i.e. crunch and structural integrity) from any vegetable other than a potato. BUT these little guys do a pretty fucking good job at imitating chips. They are crunchy and tasty, plus this recipe is impossible to cock up. Get them into you, they're a ripper snack, or a fabulous side to a steak.

DO IT

1 Preheat your oven to 200ºC (fan-forced).

2 Pour the oil into a large bowl.

3 Throw the sweet potato in and give it a little tossing.

4 Then sprinkle on the tapioca flour (and any seasonings if using) and shake the fuck out of the bowl to coat all the chips in the flour. It'll get kind of sticky and weirdo but don't stress, that sticky shit is going to turn from revoltingly disturbing to cruncherific.

5 Spread the chips onto a baking tray lined with baking paper. Spread them out so they're not touching too much and all get a fair chance to crunch up.

6 Bake for about 25 minutes. Look for them turning golden brown. Turn them at the halfway point if you give enough of a fuck. I don't.

7 While they're baking, mix up the Limey Mayo. All you have to do is put the ingredients in an adorable little bowl and stir.

8 When your chips are cooked, find yourself a giant sack of salt and make it rain sodium chloride all over those chips.

9 Dip those bad boys in the Limey Mayo and give yourself a little congratulatory fondle.

Serves 2

1 tablespoon oil (whatever you like. I like to use melted duck fat because I'm a fucking legend. Olive oil is also great)

1 sweet potato, peeled and cut into chips

1 tablespoon tapioca flour

Optional flavouring – I go bonkers for chopped rosemary, cumin or chilli flakes

Salt, fuckloads of it

THE LIMEY MAYO BIT

Big ol' squeeze of Kewpie mayonnaise

Lime juice to taste

Cheeky sprinkle of cumin and pepper

PARMESAN CRACKERS

By now you know that I have no tolerance for flaccidity. So many healthy crackers are limper than a penis that is attached to a man witnessing a vagina transition from a penis holster to a baby cannon (the phenomenon otherwise known as childbirth). Yep, that's some flaccid shit. Biting into a listless cracker is sickening and I would never set you up for that sort of disappointment – these crackers are crunchy as fuck. They are basic to make, although they get a 'two fucks' rating because the dough is a bit of a cunt to roll out and slice. But if they could behave themselves for the rolling and cutting process, they would score a 'one fuck' rating. They're winners – full of fibre, omega-3 fats and crisper than your undies after three days of camping. They're also low-carb but as if we give a fuck.

DO IT

1 Heat up the oven to 200°C (fan-forced).

2 Smoosh all the ingredients together (either by stirring or with your hands). It will stick like shit to a blanket but proceed regardless, keep going until it's a consistent sticky sludge.

3 To roll it out, plonk the mixture between two pieces of baking paper. Then roll the fuck out of it. You want to roll it pretty damn thin, I'm talking thinner than Matthew McConaughey was in Dallas Buyers Club. Uh-huh, that's right, real fucking thin. You want it to be just a few millimetres thick.

4 Remove the top piece of baking paper and slice the dough into crackers.

5 Spread the crackers out so the little fuckers have room to breathe. Lift the baking paper that is acting as a hammock for the crackers and transfer onto a baking tray. Cook for 8–10 minutes. Look for a golden brown colour and the edges starting to darken.

6 Cool them on a rack.

7 Store in an airtight container. They last about a week, then they start to get a bit shit.

Makes about 50

1 cup flaxseed meal (find this in the health food aisle of the supermarket)

⅓ cup (25 g) parmesan cheese, that super finely grated stuff that looks like powder

½ cup (125 ml) water

Salt to taste, I use about ¼ teaspoon

Flavouring options – dried rosemary, pepper, garlic powder, onion powder, mixed dried herbs, sesame seeds, lemon rind, balsamic vinegar

FRUIT'N'NUTS

I'm a bit of cheeky fucker for calling this a recipe. It's just one thing smeared on another thing, but it's a damn tasty trick to have up your sleeve when you've got the munchies. Sweet crunchy apples are the perfect vehicle but I also like to do this with bananas. It's such a pleasing zero-fucks situation, plus it reminds me of a dear friend who used to chase me around our share house with peanut butter smeared on a strap-on. She even answered a knock at the door while wearing dear old 'Strappy' once and was rather partial to rolling the bin out with him on. Ahhhhh, beautiful memories that will last a lifetime. A good smear campaign doesn't necessarily have to involve peanut butter – this trick also works a fucking treat with sliced peach smeared with soft Persian feta.

DO IT

1 Smear the nut butter on the fruit.

2 *Finis.*

Serves 1

1 apple or banana, sliced

1 tablespoon peanut butter (or almond butter, hazelnut spread, etc.)

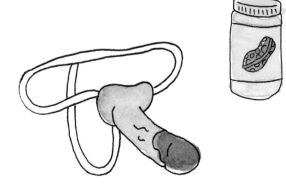

CHOCOLATE CHIP COOKIES

I grew up in the age of treats. Attended the supermarket with your mother and refrained from knocking over an entire display of sauce with a trolley? Got yourself a treat. Got bullied at school and didn't retaliate with crotch kicks or resorting to calling them a fuckstick/doodlebug/douchenozzle/dickbeetle/ballbag/penis-sniffer/fuck-knuckle/dick-arse/douche-baguette/fluffnoggin/dickbreath/fucklet/deadshit/cheese-dick/fuckface/tool/dicknose? Got yourself a treat. Turned off Teenage Mutant Ninja Turtles when told to? Got yourself a treat. Watched that potty mouth around your grandparents? That's right, kid, you got yourself a fuckin' treat. So here I am. A grown up, programmed to work for treats. These Chocolate Chip Cookies are kinda healthy because they contain a fuckload of oats, but they still count as a fucking rad treat.

DO IT

1 Preheat your oven to 180°C (fan-forced).

2 Whack the oats in a food processor and whizz them until they look fine and powdery.

3 Then add in everything else, except the chocolate chips, and whizz again.

4 Next, stir through the chocolate chips.

5 Let the dough sit on the bench for at least 20 minutes – it firms up like a fluffed dick, which makes it way easier to ball up.

6 Make the cookies – ball up bits of dough into golf ball size, place them on a baking tray lined with baking paper. Squash slightly.

7 Bake for 10–15 minutes, look for them turning golden brown.

8 Gently place them on a cooling rack – be tender as fuck so they don't fall apart. Once they're cool, they're tough and crunchy and bloody delicious.

Makes about 10–12

2 cups (180 g) rolled oats

½ cup (120 g) softened butter or coconut oil

⅓ cup (80 ml) honey or maple syrup (I use half/half)

1 egg

1 tablespoon vanilla extract

½ teaspoon salt

¾ cup (120 g) chocolate chips (I just use the dirty ones, but you can cut up raw chocolate if you want to be knobby)

SNICKERS SLICE

Back at the tender age of 18 when I moved to the big city, I lived with a best mate around the corner from a Bi-Lo supermarket. We made many happy memories in that store. Like the time my mate asked me from the other end of the Health & Beauty aisle, 'Shan! Do you need more Anusol?', or further down the same aisle on another day, 'Look! 3-ply toilet paper! So you won't put your fingers through it anymore!' The manager was a lovely gent, who took our frequent, menacing acts of ridiculousness in his stride. Fifteen years after this harassment, the manager ended up moving to my home town and becoming friends with my mum. Imagine my horror as I contemplate whether he has blocked out hearing me take over the loudspeaker asking for a price check on VagiClean. In those silly days my trolley contained M&Ms, sausages, bread and Snickers. Now I make healthier versions like this fucking delicious Snickers Slice and I tend not to publicly embarrass myself quite so often. Well, I try.

DO IT

1 Give the nuts a pulse in a food processor to crush them, then set them aside for later.

2 Throw the base ingredients into the food processor and whizz the shit out of it.

3 Smoosh into the base of a greased or lined slice tin (20 cm square) and sprinkle the crushed nuts on top.

4 Now mix your Choccie Topper together and pour it on top.

5 Whack this shit in the fridge to chill for a few hours, then slice it up. Store it in the fridge or it'll get weird.

Makes about 16 pieces

THE BASE BIT

1 cup (280 g) peanut butter

½ cup (175 g) honey

1 teaspoon vanilla extract

½ teaspoon salt

2 cups (180 g) rolled oats

¼ cup flaxseed meal

1 tablespoon coconut oil

THE NUTTY BIT

1 cup (about 150 g) macadamias, roasted and salted. You can use peanuts instead to save cash. Did I mention they need to be roasted and salted?! Because they absolutely fucking do

THE CHOCCIE TOPPER

1 tablespoon maple syrup or honey

3 tablespoons (60 ml) melted coconut oil

¼ cup (25 g) cacao powder

A bee's dick of salt

GENUINE IMITATION MINT SLICE

I grew up in a little town called Yarrawonga. Despite being an ugly little nerd, I enjoyed being a kid. I had a pony called Finn who was one of the loves of my life. He was a naughty little fucker, he was shiftier than Bill Cosby. But he was my best chum. We'd swim in the Murray River, roar around the bush tracks, gallop beside the highway racing cars (sorry Mum) and he even gave me 'kisses' – brushing his soft velvet muzzle against my face. Sometimes his kisses were tender and gentle, done just for love. Other times they were delivered because he'd seen I was carrying a honey sandwich, his favourite treat, and then the kisses would become forceful and pointed: 'Give me the fucking sandwich!' It wasn't only ponies that got treats in Yarrawonga, it was kids too. Mum and Dad used to keep a packet of Mint Slice biscuits in the fridge, and I used to love getting my trotters in there, making a cuppa and enjoying a Mint Slice or two. And by two I mean seven. So this recipe is a salute to those minty fuckers. When you look at the list of ingredients, I can understand you saying, 'Fuck you, Shannon, and that shifty piece of shit pony you rode in on', but don't be put off. It is so easy.

DO IT

1 To make The Base, simply chuck all that shit in a food processor and give it a razzin'. Keep giving it shit until it looks fine and sticky.

2 Line a slice tin (a square 20 cm tin or something similar) with baking paper then press the base mixture firmly in. Make it nice and flat, then pop it in the fridge while you make the next bit.

3 To make The Minty Bit, put the cashews, coconut oil, maple syrup and peppermint essence into the food processor and set to 'fucking max power' and blitz until it looks kind of creamy.

4 Now plonk that layer onto the base layer and smooth it out, then back in the fridge it goes while you make The Choccie on Top.

5 That part is easy as piss too. Just stir all the ingredients in a little bowl until it's nice and even.

6 Now you can pour the chocolate on top of your creation and whack that fucker in the fridge again to cool its jets and firm up. After a few hours it'll be ready to slice up.

7 Store these tasty little bastards in the fridge.

Makes about 16 pieces

THE BASE

3 tablespoons cacao powder

2 cups desiccated coconut

1 cup almond meal

¼ cup (60 ml) maple syrup

¼ cup (60 ml) coconut oil

A bee's dick of salt (let's be more precise and say ¼ teaspoon)

THE MINTY BIT

1 cup (150 g) raw cashews, soaked in water for at least a few hours, then drained

½ cup (120 ml) coconut oil

4 tablespoons maple syrup

2 teaspoons peppermint essence

THE CHOCCIE ON TOP

1 tablespoon maple syrup

3 tablespoons (60 ml) melted coconut oil

4 tablespoons cacao powder

A pimple on a bee's dick portion of salt

MY MOTHER-IN-LAW'S CHOCOLATE BALLS

My mother-in-law makes these for me all the time. What do you think is the number one ingredient? Poison? Her tears of disapproval? Laxatives? You likely had it right the first time, it probably is poison. But these little balls are so bloody tasty I'll risk a slow paralysing death just to get them in and around my mouth. Yeah, nahhhhhhhhhhh, she wouldn't poison me! Sure, she'd be rid of me for good, and her grandsons would probably turn out to be more refined citizens, but Mr Shannon would regularly be out on patrol for fresh beaver and her babysitting duties would go off the charts. She knows it's not a wise move. Plus, she's actually a ripper – at Christmas she served me a piece of chocolate cheesecake cut out in the shape of a cock'n'balls and when I just couldn't squeeze it in my already overstuffed Chrissie tummy, she said, 'How about just the tip?' I adore her. Her Chocolate Balls are delicious and super easy to make – they're my second favourite set of balls she's ever produced.

DO IT

1 Whack all the ingredients into a food processor and whizz the fuck out of it.

2 Then roll them into balls with your bare hands like a sexy beast, and roll them in the extra coconut to give them that lovely pubey coating which stops them sticking to each other.

3 Whack them in the fridge to set. Store in the fridge and enjoy these little knackers.

Makes about 12

12 Medjool dates, pitted

⅓ cup (80 ml) coconut oil

⅓ cup (35 g) cocoa or cacao powder

1 cup (120 g) almond meal

½ cup (40 g) desiccated coconut

1 tablespoon chia seeds

Plus extra desiccated coconut to roll these bad boys in

EASY AS FUCK CHOCOLATE CAKE

I wish I'd had this cake when I was a dumbfuck 19 year old. I had been scallywagging with friends, and like a pack of knobs, we decided we would be total bad-arses and smoke a cheeky joint or five. It left me with a severe case of the munchies. There was a bag of marshmallows in the pantry, and I got my trotters stuck right into them. Things didn't turn out so ace. My little country rig wasn't used to the sins of the big city and I ended up hanging over the bathtub, spewing fluffy clouds of doom. So, say no to drugs, kids. Or at least don't be a huge dickbeetle and eat an entire bag of marshmallows afterwards. It would be much more sensible to try this Easy as Fuck Chocolate Cake instead, it's much gentler on the tum.

DO IT

1 Preheat the oven to 160°C (fan-forced).

2 Pop the dry stuff (almond meal, cacao powder, baking powder and salt) in a large bowl and stir it all around like a crazy fuckwit.

3 Then add in all the wet ingredients (the oil, milk, maple syrup, yoghurt and eggs) and get your crazy fuckwit stir happening again. The batter will be quite thick but don't stress, she'll be apples.

4 Grease yourself a 20 cm round cake tin and line it with baking paper.

5 Spoon the batter into the tin and smooth it out, leaving a wee dint in the middle so the centre doesn't rise like Jesus.

6 Bake it in the oven for about 35–40 minutes. Keep an eye on that fucker though because almond meal turns on you.

7 Leave it in the tin for 5 minutes, then turn it out and let that baby cool on a cake rack.

8 To make the icing, simply mix all the ingredients together then pour that shit on the cake. Don't do it when the cake is hot as fuck or it'll just melt like Kris Jenner's face would in the rain. Place in the fridge to set the icing a little, it's pretty gooey.

Serves about 10

THE CAKE

3 cups (360 g) almond meal

⅓ cup (35 g) cacao powder

2 teaspoons baking powder

½ teaspoon salt

½ cup (125 ml) melted coconut oil (or butter)

½ cup (125 ml) milk (coconut, cow, whatever)

⅓ cup (80 ml) maple syrup

¼ cup (70 g) plain yoghurt (or dairy-free coconut yoghurt)

4 eggs, lightly beaten

THE GOOEY ICING

⅓ cup (90 g) tahini

⅓ cup (80 ml) maple syrup

2 tablespoons cacao powder

1 teaspoon vanilla extract

¼ teaspoon salt

LUNCHBOX CHOCOLATE CAKES

FUCKS GIVEN

TASTINESS

Most of my fancy-pants healthy cakes contain nuts, which is entirely unhelpful if you have school-age children because chances are you are not allowed to pack nuts in the lunchbox. There is a very solid reason for this – because some poor fucker with a nut allergy may die. While you might privately think these allergy kids are total Milhouse Van Houten material, that opinion is irrelevant. Serious allergic reactions are bonkers: tissues swell, suffocation begins, hearts practically explode. Avoiding this is fucking important. If you've ever wondered what it feels like to have an anaphylactic allergic reaction, try this: 1) Shove cotton wool down your throat to get that super fun 'can't fucking breathe' feeling; 2) If you have a vagina, nestle a large portion of ham amongst your labia. Because every mucus membrane swells, even your loin-chops; 3) Sticky-tape your eyes shut; 4) Remove your undies. Use a soup ladle to pour oozey faeces directly into them; 5) Spin around repeatedly like a dog scratching its arse on the carpet until you fall over; 6) Die quietly. So don't be a douchenozzle, don't pack nuts in the lunchbox. Some other poor parent is hoping like fuck you won't be a flog and kill their little Milhouse. Try these cakes instead, you'll still be sneaking healthful ingredients into your ungrateful spawn.

DO IT

1 Preheat your oven to 170°C (fan-forced).

2 Get out a blender or food processor and add in the eggs, milk, vanilla extract, honey and dates. Blend the fuck out of that.

3 Then add in the quinoa, coconut oil, cocoa, baking powder and salt. Blend again until that lumpy shit is smooth. Have a sniff. Not fucking bad, ey?

4 Now pour that into a muffin tin, lined with those cute little paper cupcake cases.

5 Whack in the oven and bake for about 30 minutes. Look for the top cracking and the cakes being spongey but firm.

6 Allow to cool on a cake rack.

7 Make the icing by simply whipping the ingredients together with electric beaters. Smear over your dear little cakes.

8 Rejoice in the fact no Milhouses will be harmed in the schoolyard consumption of these cakes.

Makes 12 cupcakes

THE CAKEY BIT

4 eggs

¼ cup (60 ml) milk

1 tablespoon vanilla extract

½ cup (175 g) honey

10 Medjool dates, pitted

2 cups cooked quinoa (chilled)

½ cup (125 ml) melted coconut oil or melted butter, allowed to cool its jets

½ cup (50 g) unsweetened cocoa (or cacao for healthier flogs. But they can be a bit bitter with cacao)

2 teaspoons baking powder

A bee's dick of salt

THE ICING

1 ripe avocado, roughly mashed*

⅓ cup (115 g) honey

⅓ cup (35 g) unsweetened cocoa

1 teaspoon vanilla extract

* If your kids say healthy eating can go fuck itself then swap the avocado for ⅓ cup (75 g) softened butter.

FLOURLESS BLUEBERRY MUFFINS

If you think these muffins are diet food because they are flourless and contain a fuckload of fruit, then you're dreamin'. While they are nutritious, if you overdo it, they can still make you chubby. Personally, I am open to a bit of chub. Carrying a few extra kilos has never seemed to interfere with my ability to obtain quality dick. I've crunched the numbers and determined that being a bit lighter won't make me happier, healthier or more full of semen, so I'm not going to be saying no to cake any time soon for the sake of a thigh gap and exposed ribs. Especially when cake is as tasty as this. Every time I eat these Blueberry Muffins I get so excited I have to pop a napkin in my panties to ensure I'm not leaving a snail-trail behind me.

DO IT

1 Preheat the oven to 180ºC (fan-forced).

2 Get that trusty food processor out and load that fucker with the apples, maple syrup, vanilla extract, coconut oil and eggs. Set it to 'Going Off My Tits' mode and whizz the shit out of it all.

3 Add in the oats and give them a whizz so they're broken up and won't offend any health-averse knobs.

4 Pop in the almond meal, baking powder and salt and whizz again to combine.

5 Now you need to stir in the blueberries. You can't trust your food processor with this job, he's too much of a cutty motherfucker.

6 Spoon the mixture into a muffin tray lined with paper cases.

7 These little champs will cook in about 20 minutes but, as with all things almond meal, keep an eye on these cheeky sons of bitches – they'll burn if you give them half a chance.

Makes about a dozen

2 apples, peeled, cored and chopped

⅓ cup (80 ml) maple syrup

2 teaspoons vanilla extract

⅓ cup (80 ml) coconut oil
(or soft butter)

4 eggs

1 cup (90 g) rolled oats

2 cups (240 g) almond meal

2 teaspoons baking powder

1 teaspoon salt

1 cup (150 g) frozen blueberries

MICROWAVED CAKE FOR ONE

I'm an emotional eater. Apparently it's not healthy behaviour but I personally think there are much worse coping mechanisms. Like heroin. Or punching people's faces/throats/genitals. Or public masturbation. So, while not ideal, dabbling in a cheeky bit of comfort food isn't a big deal to me. Plenty of health bloggers love to offer advice on curing emotional eating. 'Eat only when you're REALLY hungry!' *Haha. Ok, great.* 'Try taking a bubble-bath!' *Why? Are the bubbles edible?* 'Have a glass of water instead! Try flavouring it with fruit!' *Well now you've gone too far, how does 'get fucked' sound?* Drinking water and baths are great, but you know what else is great? CAKE. However, if you're anything like me it can be hard to pump the brakes. There was one occasion I made a chocolate cake and I kept going back for 'just one more cheeky sliver.' Next minute seventy per cent of the cake had been eaten. Whoopsie-doodle. That's where this cheeky minimal fucks Microwaved Cake For One comes in bloody handy.

DO IT

1 Plonk the coconut oil into a mug and heat in the microwave until melted (10–20 seconds).

2 Tip the melted oil into a small bowl or second mug (the original mug will now be well-lubed and ready to take the finished batter later on).

3 Add the egg, maple syrup, vanilla extract and milk into the coconut oil and give that shit a wee stir.

4 Now whack in the cacao, coconut flour, almond meal and baking powder. Stir the absolute bejesus out of it, and quick smart before it clumps up like a dirty shit.

5 When it's all mixed up, spoon it into the original lubed-up mug.

6 Cook it on high in the microwave for 2 minutes. Then have a peep, does it need more? If so, cook a further 10 seconds and recheck, and so on. Every microwave is a little different but they will all make a dick-sucker out of you if given the opportunity.

7 That's it, kids. You can eat it as is, or you can serve it with cream, syrup or sauce. Easy as fuck!

Serves 1 legend

2 tablespoons coconut oil
(YES. That's a fuckload, but it's necessary)

1 egg

1 tablespoon maple syrup (this isn't a super-sweet result, so if you're a mad sweet-tooth use 2)

1 teaspoon vanilla extract

2 tablespoons milk of your choice (coconut, cow, almond, soy)

2 tablespoons unsweetened cacao powder (or just normal cocoa if you're less of a knob)

½ tablespoon coconut flour

1 tablespoon almond meal

½ teaspoon baking powder

TO SERVE

Whatever the fuck you want. Maple syrup? Cream? Coconut cream? Homemade chocolate sauce? You can make your own chocolate sauce with melted coconut oil, cocoa and milk

TWO MINUTE PB&J MINI PUDDING

I remember being a kid and reading about North Americans' PB&J sandwiches in my Saddle Club books and thinking, 'You wacky Yanks!' Then, as a grown-arse woman, I tried it. Holy fucking shit, that's some tasty shit. You Americans are alright. I mean, there's maybe a few indiscretions you should sort out. Like you think a fanny is an arse/bum/poo-chute. Um, NO. A fanny is a goddamn vagina. That mix-up could lead to a lot of confusion and some very painful accidents. What if I dated an American chap and I asked him to touch my fanny and he poked a finger straight up my blowhole? That could lead to some mayhem, bloodshed and dirty fingernails. And don't get me started on your delay in embracing the metric system. Oh! And those things you call guns? We call them bingy-bangy-killy-sticks and we are not allowed to have them. But the PB&J thing is a total winner so I've used it here in this single serve pudding. Ta, mates.

DO IT

1 In a microwave-safe mug, whack in the coconut oil, and nuke it until it's melted (10–20 seconds).

2 In a second mug or small bowl, combine the egg, peanut butter, honey, milk and vanilla extract. Give it all a stir, then add in the almond meal, coconut flour and baking powder. Stir that until it's smooth. Then pour in that melted oil and stir again.

3 Now spoon in half of that peanut butter mixture into the original lubed-up mug, then spoon in the jam, then spoon in the remaining peanut butter mixture on top.

4 Cook on high in the microwave for 2 minutes.

5 Don't burn your fucking tongue on that hot as buggery jam, ok friends?

6 Feel free to celebrate with fanny touching.

Serves 1

1 tablespoon coconut oil

1 egg

2 tablespoons peanut butter

1 tablespoon honey

1 tablespoon milk (coconut, cow, almond, whatever)

1 teaspoon vanilla extract

1 tablespoon almond meal

½ tablespoon coconut flour

¼ teaspoon baking powder

2 tablespoons strawberry jam (regular jam is fine. This is a fucking treat, so a bit of processed sugar won't kill you. But if you want to be more health conscious, feel free to puree some fresh strawberries with chia seeds and heat them in a saucepan for 5 minutes for a more floggish health nerd jam)

BANANA & STICKY DATE PUDDINGS

FUCKS GIVEN

TASTINESS

Holy fuckballs! These little puddings are made from nuts, bananas, oats and eggs. That is some nutritious shit. But does this recipe have a little sugar . . .? Of course it fucking does, it's pudding. 'Why are you calling this healthy? It has maple syrup in it. Don't you know that's sugar?' asked some flog on my blog. Calm your cyber-tits! No fuckwit is trying to tell you maple syrup isn't sugar, it says syrup right there on the goddamn label. I'm no detective but that gives me a fair fucking clue there's some sugar in it. For me, healthy eating isn't about cutting bad shit out, it's about adding good shit in. Like more fruit, more wholegrains, more nuts. So what if there's a cheeky bit of sugar in your sweets? A world without genuine dessert can go fuck itself.

DO IT

1 Bang the oven on to 160°C (fan-forced).

2 Combine the bananas, dates, coconut oil, vanilla extract, eggs and maple syrup in a food processor and give it a good whizzing. Then add the chia seeds and oats and re-whizz.

3 In a large bowl, combine the almond meal, baking powder and salt.

4 Pour the juicy goo into the dry ingredients and give it a stir.

5 Divide the mixture between four ramekins (10–12 cm diameter).

6 Cook those delicious little fellas for about 35 minutes or until the top looks lightly golden, and if you insert a skewer it will come out clean despite the cakes feeling soft to the touch.

7 Make the caramel sauce while they're cooking. Melt the butter in a saucepan over medium heat, then add in the other Saucey Bit ingredients and stir until combined. Let it come to the boil, then turn it down to a simmer for a further 20 minutes.

8 Serve the individual puddings with shitloads of caramel sauce and give yourself a goddamn high five and/or whistle-touching, you've earned it.

Serves 4 (pretty big fuckers)

THE PUDDINGY BIT

2 super-ripe bananas

20 Medjool dates, pitted

⅓ cup (80 ml) coconut oil

1 teaspoon vanilla extract

2 eggs

2 tablespoons maple syrup

1 tablespoon chia seeds

½ cup (45 g) rolled oats

1 cup (120 g) almond meal

2 teaspoons baking powder

A bee's dick of salt

THE CARAMEL SAUCEY BIT

2 tablespoons butter

1 cup (250 ml) coconut milk

½ cup (125 ml) maple syrup

1 teaspoon vanilla extract

¼ teaspoon salt

HEALTHY PEAR CRUMBLE

It's not often that a healthy version of something trumps the original bad-boy, but I think this recipe comes fucking close. As kids, Mum used to cook dessert for us pretty much every night. No wonder we fucking adore her, even though she sent us to school wearing notoriously daggy, itchy, hand-knitted jumpers. She made up for accidentally making us bully magnets by cooking delicious shit like apple crumble. *What's in it, Mum?* 'Hmmn, let me see . . . sugar, flour, apples . . . and to balance out all that fruit, add a bit more sugar.' *Oh. Well, my dentist and endocrinologist would like to have a word with you, Mum. And I'm sure the Department of Human Services would like to discuss the infliction of emotional terrorism on your beloved children with those fucking jumpers. For Christ's sake, Mum, you may as well have sounded the 'Loser Alert' horn as we walked in the school gate. What were you thinking? Did you need to use up the wool that badly? Or was it punishment for making the cat wear a doll's cardigan and pushing him in a pram? Because he really liked that, Mum, he did.* Lucky the old girl can overcome any parenting fails with her tasty cooking. And so can you, friends, with this delicious but nutritious take on the humble crumble.

DO IT

1 Plonk your pears into a saucepan with the ginger, cinnamon, vanilla and apple juice, and place it over a high heat. When it starts to bubble, turn it back to a simmer and let it cook for 30 minutes with the lid off.

2 Preheat your oven to 170°C (fan-forced).

3 Make the crumble by simply whacking all ingredients into a food processor and pulse it until it looks crumbly. Don't overdo it and turn it into fucking dust – it won't take long.

4 Slop the pears into a baking dish, then top them with that tasty crumble. Leave some juice behind if it is too sloppy.

5 Bake it for about 30 minutes, then look for the top turning slightly golden brown and your nipples sparking up to medium-full erection levels.

6 Serve it up nude or feel free to whack some cream on top (I love making some by beating cold coconut cream with vanilla until it's all whippy and fabulous).

Serves about 8

THE PEARY PART

8 pears, cored and diced (I don't even bother peeling them)

2 teaspoons ginger, finely chopped

1 teaspoon cinnamon

1 teaspoon vanilla extract

1 cup (250 ml) apple juice

THE CRUMBLY PART

⅔ cup (90 g) macadamias

½ cup (40 g) desiccated coconut

¼ teaspoon nutmeg

1 cup (90 g) rolled oats

¼ cup (60 ml) coconut oil

¼ cup (60 ml) maple syrup

½ teaspoon salt

JAFFA ZERO-CHEESE CHEESECAKE

This cheesecake leaves me reminiscing over mine and Mr Shannon's engagement. The fucker had planned it beautifully. We were holidaying on a gorgeous island, he had a vintage ring, he had champagne, and had arranged for a helicopter ride to a white, sandy beach. But the night before this magical day was supposed to happen, we went out for burgers, wine and cheesecake. And we got pissed. Real pissed. We came home happy as fuck at silly o'clock, and I took my bra off, lay down and rubbed my bursting tummy. Mr Shannon's face became weird. 'Do you need a shit?' I asked him. He mumbled something and then disappeared. I assumed he went off to lay a cable that would impress Telstra. He reappeared a few minutes later and knelt beside the bed where I was laying like a bloody dugong, overstuffed with food, bubbleguts on parade. And that was the moment he chose to say, let's do forever. What a pair of flogs. I wouldn't have it any other way though, neither of us were built for romance. It was a fabulous night and it sure was a fucking fabulous cheesecake. This healthy Jaffa Zero-Cheese Cheesecake is too.

DO IT

1 Get all the base ingredients into the food processor. Tell that appliance there's no room for laziness on this team and set it to 'Turbo Super Max Power'. You might have to stop every now and then and scrape the sides down and re-rev that son of a bitch.

2 Grease a 20 cm spring-form cake tin. Smoosh all the tasty base into the bottom and make it flat, then pop it in the fridge.

3 Next you're making the topper. You might want to give the food processor a bit of a rinse (or you could be a lazy fuck like me, then you can just dump the next load in there if you're cool with brown poo-like streaks).

4 Grab your drained cashews, orange juice, orange zest, coconut cream, maple syrup, vanilla extract and coconut oil and get all that sweet shit into the food processor. Set it to 'Off-its-Tits' mode again. To make it super smooth and creamy you will have to whizz it for several minutes, with a few intermissions to scrape the sides down.

5 TIME TO UNITE BASE AND TOPPER! Get the base out of the fridge and smooth the orange goo on top, make it nice and pretty. It actually looks quite ugly, doesn't it? But you can pretty it up with melted chocolate if you give a fuck.

6 Now to play the painful waiting game. That delicious creation has to go back in the fridge to chill and set for a few hours before slicing and dicing that tasty motherfucker. Post-cheesecake engagements are optional.

Serves 8–10

THE BASE

1 cup (140 g) macadamias, roasted

1 cup (80 g) desiccated coconut

2 tablespoons cacao powder

10 Medjool dates, pitted

2 tablespoons melted coconut oil
(or melted butter)

½ teaspoon salt (if your macadamias are salted, you won't need this)

THE CHEEKY TOPPER

2 cups (300 g) raw cashews, soaked the fuck out of in water for 6+ hours (this makes them whip up smoother)

2 oranges (we'll use the zest and the juice)

½ cup (125 ml) coconut cream

¼ cup (60 ml) maple syrup

2 tablespoons coconut oil

OPTIONAL

1 teaspoon orange essence. If you want a stronger orange flavour, add this in. I don't, but you totally fucking can

Melted chocolate to drizzle on top
(I make it out of ½ tablespoon maple syrup, 1 tablespoon melted coconut oil and 2 tablespoons cacao powder)

THERE IT IS, KIDS.

THAT'S 60 RECIPES TO PLAY WITH, TO GET YOU COOKING AND GIGGLING IN YOUR KITCHEN.

I REALLY HOPE YOU FUCKING ENJOY THEM.

LOVE,

SHANNON X

GLOSSARY

A bee's dick of salt: commonly referred to in cooking circles as 'a pinch of salt'.

Back nine: your arsehole/anus/buttonhole/leather Cheerio/wazoo, i.e. 'Oh, you have vaginal thrush? That's ok, flip over and I'll play the back nine.'

Blowhole: see *back nine*. May also be used to refer to one's mouth if used for playing the skin-flute.

Bogan: Australian/New Zealand speak for an unrefined individual. Often slung in a disparaging-arsehole manner to indicate the recipient of the low-class but pejorative cunts can go fuck themselves.

Bubbleguts: a swollen belly. May be due to foetal load (human baby) or faecal load (food baby).

Buttonhole: brown sunflower/shithole/ring-piece.

Chubbies: penile erections. Related terms include boner/stiffie/ramrod/hard-on/womb-raider.

Dickbeetle: an insect distinguished by having a phallus-shaped protuberence at its proximal end; a beetle that has crawled upon a penis and hence taken on the scent and crumbs of that penis; a human that behaves like some sort of fuck-knuckle.

Dingaling: penis/skin-flute/doodle.

Doodlebug: see *dickbeetle*.

Douchenozzle: the part of a vagina-washing apparatus that enters the giney-hole; someone who is a bit of a dickhead; a flog whom you hold in contempt.

Elaine Benes: If you don't know who this important historical figure is, then find Marty McFly and get in a time machine and travel to the 90s to learn some goddamn pop history.

Flash fuck: someone with class or at least attempting to create the illusion of class.

Flog: a real wanker.

Flogchops: an individual who likes to flog their chops, i.e. pull their dick. May also refer to an individual who loves to be a story-rooster (yacks excessively) as chops also refers to the oral cavity in addition to genitalia. Australian English is breathtaking.

Freshlord: a person with fresh and fabulous views. Related terms include legend/ripper/champion/grousecunt.

Fucker: a person who will fuck with you any chance they get. Can also be used affectionately.

Fuckface: a person with a face of the fucked variety; a person with poor but strongly held views who loves to share them excessively and obnoxiously. Related terms include: fuckwit/fuck-knuckle/fucklord.

Fuckstick: a knob.

Grouse: of high quality; excellent; possessing outstanding qualities; Australian slang used almost exclusively by unassuming, awesome country mice and avoided by snobbish braggarts.

Grousecunt: an individual who is fucking grouse.

Jimmy Rowes: a revolting bar (now closed) marketed to university students and creeps, famous for cheap shots, RnB grinding music and vomit on the bathroom floors.

Jizzbucket: a derogatory term for an individual who loves the dick. Related terms include cum-dumpster/hoebag and the classics, slut/slurry/tart. Slut-shaming is for dingalings though. People want to get roots don't they? Why would they tease good reliable providers?!

Knackers: testes/balls/bollocks/nuts/coin-purse/nads.

Knob: whistle/dick/schlong/pink-pipe/cum-gun.

Knobjockey: an individual who rides knobs.

Loinchops: vulva. Related terms include fanny/giney/Captain Pinkenstein/cock pocket/beaver/meat curtains/clangers/flaps.

Milhouse Van Houtens: aka Paul Pfieffers. Nerdy individuals who are prone to excessive allergies and are often bully targets.

Pinger: Methylenedioxymethamphetamine/MDMA/an ecstasy pill. This stimulates one's central nervous system and increases sensory awareness. May also cause oneself to shit their pants, have sex with ugly people and experience a severe case of cotton mouth.

Piss-weasel: baloney-pony/cock/ding-dong/dipstick.

Pop-off: to blow the dust off a shit; a puff of gas woofed from an anus. Related terms include fart/blow-off/air-biscuit/crop-dust.

Povo: poverty stricken, i.e. 'Nah, I can't afford a sausage roll today, mate, I'm too povo.' Related terms include pov-cat.

Ring-piece: a family-friendly term for anus/sphincter ani. Related terms include buttonhole/balloon knot/brown spider/freckle/back pussy/stink portal/poo chute/dump trumpet/temple of sodom. Let us not forget the classic 'arsehole'.

Root: to engage in sexual relations.

Rootrat: an individual who frequently and indiscriminately partakes in rooting.

Shane Crawford: an Australian football player who peaked in the 90s and was simultaneously hot as fuck.

Shitstain: an unpleasant smudge/blotch/smear caused from faecal matter.

Tossbag: a wanker; one who likes to toss their own junk/genitals. I think it technically refers to a discarded used condom but language progresses/degenerates rapidly in Australia.

Wankstain: seminal fluid left unattended which was produced from a penis which has been handled by oneself to procure a climactic response. Related terms: jizz-blob, cum-patch, sprog-puddle.

THANKS TO THESE AWESOME FUCKERS

Thanks to Mr Shannon, aka Brett. You always believe I can do stuff, you make me braver. And to my beautiful boys, Jack and Herbie, you're such good kids and I LOVE YOU!

Thanks to my Shoot Dream Team: Karina Duncan, the greatest food stylist in the world; Michael Woods, the incredible photo-man; Caitlin Bell and Caroline Griffiths for helping me cook the food we shot. I had so much fun with you all, and you guys did an incredible job.

Evi O. and Daniel New – very special thanks to you both for designing this book with a very fucking tight deadline. You really went above and beyond. You read my mind. It was like you were inside me, in the non-dirty way.

Thanks to Katrina O'Brien for editing so quickly and picking up my whoopsie-doodles.

To Izzy Yates and the team at Penguin Random House – thank you for welcoming this ol' Clydesdale into the Penguin Random House stable and for not paying me in carrots. I appreciate your mob taking a chance on this silly book!

Thanks to Zoë Foster Blake for endorsing a book with an illustrated strap-on inside it. You have exquisite taste and I'm *very* grateful for your support. Thanks also to Jo Elvin (*Glamour UK*), Monty Dimond (*Show + Tell*), Tim Crowe (*Thinking Nutrition*) and Lauren Dubois (*The Thud*) for your encouragement and kind words. You are all inspiring and fabulous!

Thanks to Mel for sharing your family's ham recipe (thank Steve and Martina too!), for sharing your cooking prowess and for being the best mate a weirdo could dream of. I love you!

Thanks to Katey, legend and best mate, who supported me and proofread on a bloody Sunday.

Special thanks to Hayles for providing me with a plethora of ridiculous, funny memories to choose from. You are one of the funniest and most generous people ever.

Thanks to Linz for helping me realise linoleum is probably the best farting surface, and to both Linz and Lambie for being lifelong chums.

Thanks to Julie Postance for showing me how to produce a book from scratch. I would've been up shit creek without your guidance.

And Mum, thanks for your marinara recipe, proofreading, caring for my boys when I fucked my back, and for **always** letting me be 'free to be me'. I love you, Mum.

But most of all: thanks to every legend who has joined me at shannonskitchen.com. You are some funny, weird people. I can't believe we have a BOOK!

Oh, and YOU! Thanks for buying my book.

SHANNON x

PENGUIN BOOKS

UK | USA | Canada | Ireland | Australia
India | New Zealand | South Africa | China

Penguin Books is part of the Penguin Random House group of companies
whose addresses can be found at global.penguinrandomhouse.com.

Penguin
Random House
Australia

First published by Bad Girls Media 2017
This revised edition published by Penguin Random House Australia Pty Ltd 2018

Design, typesetting and illustration by OetomoNew
Photography by Michael Woods
Food styling by Karina Duncan
Editing by Katrina O'Brien, Illustrated Publishing
Home economists: Caitlin Bell and Caroline Griffiths
Printed and bound in China by 1010 Printing International Ltd

 A catalogue record for this
book is available from the
National Library of Australia

ISBN: 978 0 14379 251 2

penguin.com.au